A PLACE OF EXODUS

BOOKS BY DAVID BIESPIEL

Republic Café
The Education of a Young Poet
A Long High Whistle
Poems of the American South
Charming Gardeners
Every Writer Has a Thousand Faces
The Book of Men and Women
Long Journey
Wild Civility
Pilgrims & Beggars
Shattering Air

A PLACE OF EXODUS
Home, Memory, and Texas

David Biespiel

Kelson Books
Portland, Oregon

Published by KELSON BOOKS
2033 SE Lincoln, Portland, Oregon 97214
kelsonbooks@gmail.com

Book and cover design by Steve Connell | *steveconnell.net*
Cover art: *Untitled*, acrylics, by David Biespiel

Kelson Books are printed on paper from certified sustainable forestry practices.

Printed in the United States of America.

ISBN 978-0-9827838-5-6

Library of Congress Control Number: 2020935326

Now these are the names of the children of Israel, which came into Egypt

Contents

THE HARD HOURS

Rubbed and Worn

I never told anyone this, but for a time I thought I would be a rabbi when I grew up. Not that I thought about it every day, but especially during my teenage years, by which time it was already too late.

Not what you'd think of when you imagine the mystique of a deep-down Texas childhood, with the cattle and pump jacks and muggy vastness, pine pollen and red dirt, farm-to-market roads stitching together lonesome towns that get hotter after the sun sets, evangelical radio, Friday night football, Lone Star flags flying over all the gas stations, eighty thousand miles of freeways and billboards, boots and belts and ten gallon hats.

But I don't know how else to describe it. Chanting Hebrew prayers inside the magnetism of Texas lore was my open range of obligation, my 254 counties of faith, my Book of Third and Long. Dots and dashes slashing across the siddur, the Jewish prayer book, were my hominy and grits, my leaves of trees budding in February, my hot bowls of chili, my Davy Crockett at the Alamo. The silky ink of Genesis and Exodus stained the flat drawl in my mouth, more gentility than twang, so that I felt paltry and sensuous, the verses cutting into the violent weather of my imagination with their multitudes—curved tropes skittering across the pages like a two-step, a deliberate memento and admonition of how human beings behave.

Since my first religious experiences were passed through blood, nothing went amiss. Even in the 1970s, in Houston, we still weren't so distant from the lesson of Auschwitz, that no one cared that Jews were being murdered. Nor were we so distant from my grandfather's shtetl childhood, in Ukraine, before the First World War, with stories of buying a cow and taking it to the *shochet*, the butcher trained under Jewish law. Everybody kept kosher in Cherniostrov. No such thing not keeping kosher. On Fridays when it was the time to *bench licht*—to bless the lights—there used to be a man who would go on the streets and holler, Time to *bench licht*! Several thousand families gathered in their small homes and lit the sabbath candles to brighten the way for the Messiah to travel on a glimmering current.

With the black prayer book open in my hands, in another era, in another part of the world, when I was a boy in Texas, I too was swept away by a strong current without knowing where it was taking me. Each word quickening like a dancer who refuses to slip away unnoticed, a folk dance performed over and over without rest in the face of all obstacles.

None of that required getting used to. I was an heir to it. Hebrew was a home that had been bequeathed. It came as naturally to my body as fingers and toes. It would have been weird not to be Jewish where I lived in Texas, or to hear someone announce he was renouncing Judaism, quitting Judaism, with no intention to practice Judaism in the future.

Yet with all this, there was something frightening about it, of disaster to come, like a portent of thunder clouds over the lowlands.

I suppose, when I thought of becoming a rabbi, what I wanted was to give myself a life of enduring myths, and I must have thought to live as a person of faith would purify my principles. I became a writer instead. No great leap.

Not that my family came from a rabbinical tradition, but we were shul people. Torah people. People who understood that the purpose of prayer was not to make appeals to God, but to offer praise. It wasn't that chanting Torah was going to deliver us, but make us worthy of being delivered.

Just as we all knew that shul was the word for the Orthodox Jews's prayer house, derived from a German and Latin word meaning school, a word that emphasizes the synagogue's role as a place of study, and just as we knew that conservative Jews typically use the word synagogue, which is a Greek translation of *Beit K'nesset* and means a place of assembly, and that Reform Jews use the word temple, because they consider every one of their meeting places to be equivalent to, or a replacement for, The Temple, in Jerusalem, we still just called all those places, shul. We were shul people. People who believed there was no bottom to the meaning of Judaism, who carefully examined Jewish life over and over, who understood there was no substitute for a thorough study of the Five Books of Moses, the Prophets, and the Writings, and all those competing commentaries that held the keys to psychological well-being, no substitute for laboring over the Talmud or Halakhah, the many Codes of Jewish Law, no substitute for studying the philosophies of Judaism, for reading Maimonides and Rashi and keeping a weather eye on the writings of contemporary scholars that, each generation, translate the words — someone will correct me here to say, translate the truths — of the Jewish faith into a modern idiom, grappling with contemporary questions. There would be no substitute for studying the history of the Jewish people, with those internal and external challenges for three thousand years, including defeats and victories, suffering and redemption.

We were shul people who were expected to show up, mornings or evenings, Fridays or Saturdays, at shul. They were called services, and we understood why. We knew the *She'ma* is a prayer that affirms God's unity and the *Amidah* deals with repentance and the restoration of Israel. We knew the extra blessings for celebrating the beginning of a new month and special holidays. When *Aleinu* comes in the evening *Ma'ariv* service and when it comes in the morning *Shacharit* service — and again in *Musaf*, the extra service, and yet again in *Minchah*, the afternoon service.

In shul, when I was a boy, I held my skinny body in the Southland of Jewish identity with concentration. Like a tumbleweed, I cantered heel to toe, the Hebrew soft as wind in my mouth.

We ask, where are you from? The question is a way of finding out, what separates you from me? What distinguishes you before you got wherever you are that isn't where you're from? Who were you before you were this person? What is the landscape and the weather, the outlook and spirit, ambience or disposition, from where you began your journey? What inclinations make up the very source and provenance of you, the raw materials out of which you were made? Your imprint? Your cause?

To search your past is to organize a series of queries about yourself that allow you to discover which actions and events, what behaviors and decisions, have led you to ask those very questions. Each question begs another question. Your history gets unravelled. With it, the histories of the people you shared your past with.

Because I grew up in Meyerland, the historic Jewish section of Houston, and because I left at the age of eighteen after a public quarrel with one of the city's leading rabbis, Jack Segal, who'd been my rabbi since I was four years old, and because I have had almost no contact for decades with most anyone down there, because I left that community and never returned, never called, not so much as mailed a postcard, I often have a bout of trepidation about going, well, home. Since 1982, I've been back to Meyerland but two or three times. It's always been in passing, and always accompanied by a feeling that carries me right to the edge of dread, fatigue, hostility, and dissolution.

Still, I love being an expatriate Texan. Texas holds the landscape, if not the mise-en-scène, of my true spirit. I miss the bright, massive skies, the swarming parade of clouds chasing

the wind for miles and miles. I see nothing wrong with barbecue ribs for breakfast. My go-to cookbook is the *Homesick
Texan Cookbook*, with recipes for pickled okra and chicken-
fried steak and buttermilk pie. My oldest brother lives in Texas,
on a ranch. My ninety year old father lives in Texas.

And yet, the few times I have passed through, passed
through Meyerland that is, I find myself, with no effort at all,
able to see into my old homeland something like a sequence of
moments, the map of a private history, from which I quickly
and, to my mind, dangerously retrieve my ex-self, with all
the old disaffection, fear, knowledge of death, scent of beauty,
reflections on difficult thoughts, wonder against righteousness,
and curiosity against survival, until, finally, at last, I find myself
settled into a great sadness.

But for whom or what?

I often get the question when I tell people I'm from Texas,
"There are Jews in Texas?" Yes. A lot. The storied Weequahic
section of Newark in Phillip Roth's novels has got nothing on
Houston's Meyerland, which sits on a flood plain along Brays
Bayou southwest of downtown, bound geographically by two
historic synagogues. The first is Beth Yeshurun, the largest conservative congregation in North America, where some twenty
five hundred families belong, including mine when we lived
on Loch Lomond, an integrated block of Jews and Christians,
after my father, mother, two older brothers, and I moved from
Tulsa in 1968, the year I turned four, so my father could run a
small garbage company on Wilmington Street owned by my
grandfather on my mother's side. The wood-paneled sanctuary
at Beth Yeshurun seats a thousand congregants. There's a nursery school and Day School and classrooms for Torah study,
all of which I attended. A chapel for morning and evening
minyan, and another for weekly services. A Jewish museum.
Hotel-sized kosher kitchen.

Three miles west along the bayou is the reform Temple Beth Israel, the oldest congregation in Texas history, where another two thousand families belong. Inside or adjacent to the neighborhood are Jewish high schools, smaller reform temples and conservative synagogues, as well as Orthodox and Sephardic congregations. Across the bayou from Beth Israel, taking up an entire block with its swimming pools and gymnasiums and health clubs, arts rooms and theater, dance studios and auditoriums, is the white colonnade Jewish Community Center that appears always to be cooling, like a birthday cake, in the smeared heat.

More than most neighborhoods in Houston, recently Meyerland has been nearly swept away by three catastrophic floods. Ten inches of intense rainfall over ten hours fell during Memorial Day weekend in 2015 and flooded some seven hundred homes. Three people drowned, including an older married couple—the wife's body was discovered next morning in Brays Bayou, but the husband's drifted all the way to the Port of Houston and was not discovered for nearly two days. During the Tax Day Flood of April 2016 some eight inches of rain flooded Meyerland. Another thousand homes were damaged. Then, in the summer of 2017, Hurricane Harvey crashed the Texas coastline, moved inland, then stalled, causing it to produce more than fifty inches of rain over several days in one of the highest populated areas of the U.S. Gulf Coast, the worst flood in Texas history. Major highways around Houston were shut down for days. Floodwaters overflowed bridges. People set up tents on rooftops, while others motored dinghies as rescue boats through the flooded interstates to help victims evacuate their cars or homes. Makeshift aid stations sprang up in parking lots outside strip malls. Household debris was piled head-high on streets for months. Hundreds of thousands of homes were left uninhabitable. The hurricane claimed over a hundred lives. So many families, I'm told, have had to move out of their ruined homes in Meyerland that at nighttime, with electricity cut off, street after street, from Willowbend to Beechnut, is pitch dark, as if Meyerland is the latest Jewish shtetl to be wiped off the map.

My wife, Wendy, says, *Where are you from?* is her favorite of the icebreaker questions because the range of options, such as a neighborhood, a town, a continent, is gentle. Gentler than the answers to that other icebreaker, the rude insertion, *What do you do?*

Wendy's answer is, I live in Portland, but I'm from Springfield, Oregon, in Lane County. Unincorporated Lane Country, I chime in. To which she retorts, Yes, well, you're a Texan who's lived in a dozen states and inhabited the same two liberal zip codes in Southeast Portland for more than twenty years.

She's hurt that her daughters, Ruby and Violet, when asked where they're from, say, Portland—where they were born—and not Springfield, where Wendy's mother, father, sister, niece, nephew, aunts, uncles, and cousins have lived. Portland is also the answer my son, Lucas, gives. He was two years old when we moved here, but he was born in rural Maryland, outside Washington, DC, when I lived there with his mother, my first wife, on a small ranch. Lucas's mother is Canadian. Once, about six years old, during breakfast in the clapboard house we lived in near Hawthorne Boulevard in Portland, Lucas announced over a plate of scrambled eggs and fried potatoes, I get it, I'm half Canadian, half Oregonian, half Jewish, and half Texan.

For many people, the kind who might read this book, that is, the question about where are you from begins with how people define home. One definition of home is, it's a place you think you can always go back to because it's as much a pushpin location on a map as it is embedded in your consciousness.

The decision to leave home—when it is a decision, as it was for me—perhaps indicates a breach between self and other, a fissure, a crevice. Where we are from is an opening inside us.

No matter what, consciously or subconsciously, we are clutching some shard of that place. Even if by place we mean, displaced. As James Baldwin says: "You are always the receptacle of what has gone before you, whether or not you know it and whether or not you can reach it."

Still, our understanding of what that remnant means might always be inadequate. We may never integrate our disquiet with our living selves.

We hadn't been living long on Loch Lomond in Houston when I realized I was growing up to the sound of ticking that followed a telephone ringing before dawn, belling from the kitchen. It rang through the living room, dining room, den, and into my bedroom down the hall at the edge of the one-story brick house. My parents had a phone in their room, and my father would answer and say to hold on. He'd put on a bathrobe and walk from the bedroom into the kitchen, the room so full of night even the clock on the wall could not be read. On the line was Woodrow Griffith, a truck driver from the garbage company. A front-loader had broken down.

Some mornings my father would step outside into the roaring heat with the insects chittering and sit in the car parked outside my window so not to wake anyone in the house. Using the two-way radio mounted underneath the dashboard, he would speak to Mr. Griffith about repairing the broken-down truck. The static squawked on and off against the silence over the flat lawn and spiky hedges, flowering lavender, roses and tulips, spreading oak trees, and, near the front porch, a clump of lonely pine trees.

I was five years old when we moved into the house on Loch Lomond. That first day I led our black-faced boxer Velvet up and down the street of mid-century ranch houses, with the two of us sniffing at the grass. This was a time, before leash laws, when dogs roamed around the front yards a lot. Velvet was stocky, not yet four years old, bounding ahead of me over the clean driveways, lunging back across the lawns, like a light on four paws. By mid-morning she had wandered to the end of Loch Lomond. Quick as a glimpse, she turned onto Manhattan Street and disappeared. I ran after, calling, and found her trotting into a hot wind. Nosing her way from grass blade to grass blade, she ran hard toward the sound of my voice.

After my father moved out of that house on Loch Lomond, living across Chimney Rock Road in the Nob Hill Apartments, my mother had taken over running the garbage business as if taking over a pain. I was a teenager by then. Again, before first light, the phone would ring. A truck was stalled on FM 1960. Mother's voice moved around the house and into the brightness behind the curtains. The day's first light rested in the hallways like a springy spider. Crickets and katydids and cicadas and grasshoppers ticking in the grass and trees.

M y grandfather was a haftorah man.

Haftorah is the section from the Prophets chanted in Hebrew in shul on Shabbat, following the weekly Torah reading, and during certain holidays. Most people need months of preparation to do a single haftorah portion. My grandfather could chant any portion cold, as if he had written the verse himself. Whispering into his ear on a Saturday morning where he sat about halfway up the rows of plush seats at his shul in Tulsa, B'nai Emunah, was a blue-suited usher with thinning hair and small eyes. Could you fill in today, Joe? he asks. Short notice, he says. Sure, sure. No problem, my grandfather says, not even uncrossing his legs. On Yom Kippur he chanted *Maftir Yonah*, the last and most important haftorah section of the holiday. Leaning his face over the reading table on the bimah and the pages of the *chumash*, the Torah in print form, he sang with a tender rasp that seemed to reach the fringes of the shul, the words silver out of his mouth. Up and down the aisles, the meanings of faith would open and fly like doves slowly uncoiling overhead, while all of us from our seats followed along in our heavy prayer books. After a time his soft voice ceased clinging to the shrine of the passage but seemed to carry the pilgrimage of his heart, as if he were holding God and human experience in a single melody about the ease or hardness of life, not just going along for the ride in the presence of God, but offering a testament for the momentary and the eternal, until the melody faded. When he returned to his seat, buttoning his suit jacket and tugging at his large, white-fringed tallit slung over his shoulders, from every corner of the shul men rushed to shake his hand.

I could not imagine growing up to be anything but like my grandfather, especially in shul, praying on one foot and then the other, knowing words to prayers from heart, filling in as needed—sure, sure, no problem—as if the minutes of my life were already rubbed and worn.

With his mother and younger brother, my grandfather had come from Ukraine to America through Ellis Island in 1920 as a thirteen-year-old boy—after the Russian Revolution proved to be more dangerous to Jews than its Russian Jewish advocates had predicted—and they reunited with my great-grandfather, who'd come to America ten years earlier and worked as a wagon peddler in northern Iowa, selling furs, animal hides, wool, scrap, grease, anything he could find to make a living. Venturing out on his own my grandfather built a scrap yard in Tulsa after the Second World War. In the 1950s he installed the first shear in the Southwest, a machine that took just seven minutes to reduce seven thousand pounds of heavy steel from an automobile frame into neat, two-foot length bales.

As a boy I rushed to be near my grandfather's side whenever we were together, especially when we visited Tulsa—say, a summer Shabbat evening in the house on East 38th Street. It was a dinner with parents and grandparents and great-grandfathers, aunts and uncles, grandsons and great-grandsons. Here's a room where everybody believes that the relationship between Sabbath observance and Jewish knowledge is not to be taken lightly. Here's a room where you're told by no one in particular, but by everyone there, by their stature and bearing, that Jews who discard Shabbat or give it only token attention risk becoming Jewishly ignorant, regardless of all the other Jewish activities in which they might participate.

Before dinner—roasted chicken with rosemary and raisin-spiced rice, cooked cabbage, and squares of kugel that seemed like it would never go away, and the kitchen smelling like spiced apples—we stood behind high-backed chairs and raised our slender wine glasses, with the red wine shifting from lip to lip, while Grandpa Joe, in coat and tie, his shoulders heavy and shuddering, sang the Kiddush to thank God for offering these hours as an inheritance. The words lifted through the open windows into the speckled sky like an ancient bird looking for a branch to rest on.

All evening in that dining room, in that two-story house, inside the small Jewish community of that city where my parents grew up, the adult talk goes round and round the long table, starting and stopping, and all the yarmulke'd little boys—my two older brothers and two older cousins and me dispersed among parents not our own—crawl under the table switching seats.

After dinner, in the feathered Friday night darkness, my grandfather liked to tell his tales, little sketches really, of shtetl life or coming to America. About how his mother, no matter what, managed to get something special for food for Shabbat, potatoes, or soup and potatoes, something like that, or a piece of herring with bread. About sneaking onto a boxcar with his mother and little brother alongside sleeping Polish soldiers. About the three of them riding in a huddle out of the train depot all the way to Kiev. About a new conductor coming on who starts hollering, you know, dirty Jews, get off, but a Polish officer in the boxcar, when he heard all that, he got up and he told the conductor, he says, these people are going to stay here and if you say something right now I'm going to kill you. Just said it out of the blue sky, my grandfather says, probably felt sorry for us, you know, practically naked, barefoot. Just our clothes on, he says, no shoes, no nothing. And we probably looked like hell, scared.

After dinner, with dishes cleared away, Papa Harry and Grandpa Joe—father and son, wagon peddler and scrap man—moved their chairs close to each other and *benched*, singing the set of Hebrew blessings after a meal. Whoever wanted to join did so. I see myself: a five year old boy standing beside his grandfather and looking over his shoulder at the opened prayer book, my small hand tugging the sleeve of his suit jacket.

One afternoon in the Old City in Jerusalem, during the last days of 1976, when I was twelve years old, my grandfather and I were standing next to a bazaar that sold flags and menorahs and prayer beads and crucifixes. Idolatrous crowds were pressing noisily behind us.

—How's about we do your bar mitzvah right now? The two of us. You know the prayers already. Not like at home. No speeches. We read from Torah. Few minutes. Done. That's the bar mitzvah, he said, and pressed the point that it would just be the two of us, that we'd slip away for a few hours from my parents, brothers, aunts, uncles, and cousins, and everyone else on the family trip.

—What about next year in Houston?

—That's for your friends. Here, you and me.

For months I'd been preparing my Torah and haftorah portions for my bar mitzvah at Beth Yeshurun, where I'd been attending the Day School since I was four. Practicing, I raced through the tropes with swift purpose—each word let me plunge into another, intoxicated by the whole. Slow down, said my teacher—a disheveled Holocaust survivor, dressed in suit and tie, who mumbled through his long, wrinkled face. Slow down, son, slow down. For sure I was not one of those students who spent my preparation in a passionate frenzy of learning. I wasn't one of those people who seemed a mythic student, people who scarcely left their room, ate meals standing up so as not to lose time, memorized their part unceasingly, without a break, seldom sleeping. I didn't need to cram my days full of study, and so my teacher didn't remind me not to overdo it. Didn't advise me to take a break, to set a day aside each week to go out and play in the air. Truth is, after eight years attending the grade school at the shul, none of it was difficult.

Nothing much happened next, or nothing seemed to happen. At first my grandfather and I simply threaded our way through the crowds of tourists at the Western Wall of the Temple at the Kotel tunnels until we arrived down a long flight of stairs outside the Hall of Prayer. In contrast to the languid streets and endless sidewalks of Meyerland with slender brick houses and manicured lawns with heavy oaks and magnolias, the ancient architecture in the Old City was squeezed, rubble and all, into this most holy of Jewish places—with milling crowds, and security guards in army fatigues looking bored with their automatic rifles slung over their shoulders. The Western Wall was a place of transformative possibilities, that's what we were taught, that inside all that stacked stone were so many Jewish motifs in one place: vulnerability, fortitude, wreckage, promise. To say nothing of the two mosque domes, one gold, the other silver, balancing in the background. To say nothing of the tourists partitioned from the worshippers, the men from the women.

Soon as we entered the limestone weave of corridors of the Kotel tunnels, my grandfather handed me a black yarmulke. While I rested it on the back of my head, he put on his tallit and tefillin and stepped away to find someone to help us. I listened to the buzz of praying voices, the low mumbles. Gathered around opened scrolls, some men were beating a palm against their hearts or covering their eyes. Some rocked soothingly on their heels. Others leaned against the medieval walls, their mouths fluttering in silence.

That day was six months since my grandmother's death. My mother's mother. My grandfather's wife, Ruth. Her death was one of those occasions where I began to see my life from the outside in, and it led me to begin to question the very existence of my existence.

There had been some confidence it was nothing when first my grandmother's stomach had troubled her. She came out of the bathroom while visiting us in Houston wiping her forehead and breathing hard one late morning in May, then returned to the sink and mirror to put on a touch of lipstick and dab rouge on her face. A tiny woman with fair skin that seemed to burn even in the shade, she appeared sleepy, at odds with her usual high spirits. She was sixty-four years old.

The night we buried her, the darkness in Oklahoma was thick, like an old jacket that, despite all the times it's been worn, is stiff and itchy. The moon was slender, and the house on East 38th Street was visible as a large silver stone, so many cars out front and around the block and over on the next streets. The sloping backyard where I usually played football with my brothers and cousins appeared gray. Inside the house was over-crowded, with dozens and dozens of people. A hot drowsy hum. Followed by stretches of weeping. My grandfather's face was colorless as a winter leaf. His four daughters, including my mother, huddled close in the den, all of them in hard chairs. From where I kept standing nearby, I could hear my grand-father's breathing, a tired wheeze, and he seemed to be crying without stopping. He kept his face turned downward, his chest and shoulders rising and falling.

Then he was standing to shake a hand of an adult I almost recognized.

Before the prayer service for the evening minyan took place in the crowded living room, my mouth felt slack. My eyes shapeless and heavy. I was feverish. Mother loosened my tie as we walked together into a bathroom to splash water on my face. Next, to keep me from the others, she led me upstairs to my grandmother's bed, where I removed my suit coat and shoes and tie, and was put under the covers, with several pillows stuffed close to my ribs. I could smell my grandmother's perfume in the bedcovers, and I kept rubbing my nose into the sheets, the pillow cool and moist against my cheek. After a time, I was sweating, trembling. The fever grew higher, and my breathing was at first solemn, then heavy, as I tried to sleep.

When the hallucinations started, it was like I had entered an inmost cave. At first I saw only dry branches and hard dirt. The sky hidden behind a quilt of milky clouds. There was a feast, with singing, a dusty hall paneled like a wood shed. The sun was blinding, and there was shouting. Wailing. Heavy smell of boiled potatoes. Faces flushed. Followed by laughter. Men and women hugging outside a slender house in the sunlight. Carloads of decorated Torahs stretched away toward crisscrossing train tracks.

Weightless, I drifted into more visions, brief snatches, as if each image was being inscribed on my brain. An aroma of chicken broth and perfume. A windowless room with men praying, and two birds flying out an open cage and landing on the shoulders of the praying men. Slow down, says the elder, with a high-pitched Yiddish accent, you're rushing, you're rushing, have patience. I ached from the fever. I heard voices in the hallway, shouting from the street, a dryness in my mouth, gnawing hunger, something like a dog knifing from one side of the road to the other. There was a coiling mist outside the windows, ragged, shredded.

It was impossible to know what was happening before and what after. The air in the room, furrowed from side to side, was all I had to comfort me in my grandmother's bed as I tried to sleep deeply, which finally I must have done, because when I awoke I was cold. The skin over my stomach tight. Mild darkness. A knock at the door. Footsteps. A large hand pressing across my forehead.

It was my grandfather.

He was breathing heavily through his mouth. Mother was

standing behind him, her arms crossed. You have a fever, he said. This bed's making me sick, I said, but didn't open my eyes.

For a few moments he sat at my side and began whistling a gentle tune, his right hand on my forehead. I leaned back into the pillows. Let my shoulders fall. Tried to hollow my thoughts to find some deepness to sleep inside of. For a moment I was able to look at him. His eyes were open, wet, staring into the emptiness of the room.

Death haunted my grandfather. He told harrowing tales about growing up in Cherniostrov—he needed merely a wee prompt from someone at the long dining room table after Shabbat dinner, something like, were there pogroms in the town you lived in? There weren't any pogroms in our town, he'd say. No. But there were pogroms right around us. See, there was that famous pogrom in Proskurov. They had, one Saturday afternoon, I think they must have killed a couple thousand. I do remember that they said next they were coming towards our town and so we left for Proskurov. I remember, when we got there, I think it was on Monday after all the fighting, and some of the streets there were still bloody. I remember that. But they had a pogrom in Felshtin. I don't know if there was one in Krasilov or not. You know when what's-his-name talks about Krasilov, there is a town Krasilov not too far from where we were.

Sholem Aleichem, you mean, someone reminds him, and he looks around the table of crumpled napkins, stacked dishes, and empty glasses of wine to see we're still listening.

That's right, he says. Look, we had a railroad, see. The Ukrainians were occupying our town. Okay? And the Bolsheviks were chasing them. Okay? One night, I can remember that. We lived not very far from my dad's brother. He woke us up, must have been about midnight, I don't remember. I can remember, it was *Erev Shavuot*. Summertime. My dad's brother woke us up. I was about nine or ten. He told us there was a lot of ammunition stored. The Ukrainians were going to blow it up. So the town was alerted. Nothing happened until about

nine o'clock in the morning, then the fighting started. I can remember Mother was at the market. When the shells started flying, we went to a cellar. Actually it was where they used to keep
ice. You know. We stayed there until practically in the morning
when the fighting subsided. Then we went looking for our
relatives. Must have been about, I don't know, five, six o'clock
in the morning, that the fighting started again. And there were
machine guns. We stayed there at the house. The fighting ended,
must have been about noon. That year they kept fighting. Back
and forth, back and forth, between the Bolsheviks and the
Ukrainians. Wasn't any longer than about three months that it
was a Saturday afternoon and again the fighting started. So we
head for a basement. In that time I think there must be three or
four Ukrainian soldiers came in. And first they said there were
spies in there, and all that, I guess. Then all of a sudden they
fired their rifles right into the crowd in the basement. And that's
where my aunt got killed. I was right beside her. Just a kid. The
bullet must have gone over my head and must have killed her
somehow. She died the next morning. So, all that year, practically, back and forth, back and forth.

When I think of that story now, etched like an heirloom in
my consciousness, about the pogroms of Ukraine my grandfather survived, it impresses me all the more.

Not least because, by contrast to my grandfather's hindered
childhood, I grew up as just a kid in the American South who
liked to run off and think stuff.

If on a summer's night, after Houston's petroleum-blue sky
lowered like a flag, I wandered under the hot wind, there'd be
Velvet at my side. We'd wander freely alongside the bayous into
the plaid streets with every manner of human tic and obsession
locked behind the front doors of brick houses. Here Velvet
bounds ahead, taking the scent of something, wide-eyed, her
heart on fire, happy to run, nose down. Then she lifts her head,

galloping, muscular, tearing after a yellow cat up a driveway. They both scamper toward a fence where the cat leaps over and escapes, and Velvet barks once or twice, returning to me like all of the joy in the world, but sensing my mood, picking up the rhythm of my voice and pace. C'mon, Velvet, get out of there, I call. She runs ahead under the bright lampposts, disappears, and circles around.

I knew those streets like I knew my own name. Nothing was shabby. History was a relic. There was little of a great past to be discovered. Meyerland hadn't been destroyed and rebuilt, like the bygone shtetls of Eastern Europe, or sacked by a succession of conquerors, like Jerusalem. Eavesdropping on the solitary minutes, I wasn't at risk of being caught in a pogrom. It was just a time of staying out past curfew, thinking of questions. Why do I live on my street and not on another? Where is the beginning of time and the end of time? If all things die, why not time? How much of this place is real and how much is a dream? Even Velvet seemed to pose questions with her black face tearing up patches of grass. Was I here before? Will I come back?

Is this when I first became aware that I was a separate person, that my agitations were mine? To develop a secret remove? Did that come when I would wander around the hushed streets of Meyerland, wishing to be not invisible, but abated—which has the power of perspective—taking the position of a distant spirit, looking at all things as if brightly lit?

Inside the Kotel tunnel, in the Old City in Jerusalem, at the Western Wall, in 1976, my grandfather finally returned with another man and introduced him as Mr. Avraham. Stout, bearded, with a sag in his jowls, and deep eyes, Mr. Avraham wore a large tallit wrapped around him like a bathrobe. He led us to an open table with a Torah on it, and he said something about this one scroll being good luck for your bones.

— That's the beautiful thing about prayer. Right?

— Yes, sir.

— You're lucky to have a grandfather like your grandfather. Does he need to see the prayers? Mr. Avraham said and rubbed his palm against the top of my head, causing my yarmulke to shift onto my forehead.

— I know them, I said, adjusting the yarmulke to the back of my head where I liked it, and then I recited from heart the prayer before the reading from the Torah.

When my grandfather handed me the spare tallit, I swung it over my shoulders, saying the prayer to exalt God, then held out an arm while he wrapped thin leather straps of tefillin, the small black leather cubes containing Scriptures, over my arm and forehead so that, from that hour forward, I should be preoccupied with the word of the Torah.

— It is an honor, said Mr. Avraham, shaking my hand again, and saying a verse from Hebrew from Deuteronomy.

When he let go of my hand, he instructed my grandfather to call me for bar mitzvah, which he did in Hebrew, and then in English.

— Should your heart be wise, my heart shall rejoice, and now take my instruction with you, guard it, heed it, and say, I am ready. Answer in Hebrew, son, he said.

— *Hineni*, I said.

The word means, Here I am, and the meaning evokes a readiness to act with faith. It appears more than a half dozen times in the Torah, including when Abraham says, *Hineni*, in response to God calling him out to sacrifice his son, Isaac, not to save his people or to fulfill a vow, but to prove his faith to God for its own sake, and when Jacob tricks his blind father, Isaac, into giving him and not Esau his birthright blessing, and it's what Moses says when God calls to him from the burning bush, *Hineni*, I'm ready to serve.

I watched the black letters twirl on the parchment scroll of the Torah as Mr. Avraham chanted another passage, the Hebrew letters huddling like men in fur cloaks driving a wagon from house to house in an old village, smoke rising above the huts. Each letter was shaped like a dented shul that squeezed the soil, while inside tragic, bearded men pulsated in hats without bitterness, crouched, gloomy, but with grandeur.

The back of my shirt was damp.

Mr. Avraham looked at me to say the prayer after the reading of the Torah. When I finished, we all said, Amen, shook hands, and we left.

Few families escape trouble, and in 1976 my family had a small share of it. In addition to the death of my grandmother, 1976 was the year my father suffered a life-altering stroke from which he would be severely aphasic for the rest of his life. One bright afternoon in late winter, he had been jogging easily into the last lap of a three-mile run on the small oval track on the rooftop of the Jewish Community Center on South Braeswood when a sharp pain struck behind his forehead. He smacked a palm above his eyes and stumbled against another man running alongside him, then crumpled like a rag doll onto the gravel.

The day was March 12, twenty-two days after my twelfth birthday.

Mother left her position as housewife and professional volunteer, the kind you saw in middle class Jewish families in Houston, and became the family breadwinner. What happened next was not at all unforeseen.

My parents' marriage was unhappy, and it would soon come to an end.

I don't know how my parents became close, or what love was between them when they married in December, 1957, in Tulsa. Of their marriage all I will say is that a faded newspaper portrait of them standing together that day has long lodged in my imagination.

Every wedding photo is a happy one. Foreheads close together. Shoulders touching. White tuxedo to white dress. Like two flowers planted closely in a ceramic pot. What happens later you don't see in photographs. No camera can capture it. I think they have already completed the ceremony, taken the vows at the end of a bridal pathway of white satin under an improvised altar. The canopy fashioned of Hawaiian ti leaves and white chrysanthemums.

From the newspaper clipping, from *The Tulsa World*, I have read that the twenty-two year old bride is wearing a gown of imported peau de soie fashioned with a basque bodice covered with lace embroidered with seed pearls. Her scalloped neckline is outlined with iridescent sequins, and the formal length skirt extends into a chapel train. She has pulled back her veil, adorned with medallions of lace. A heart-shaped necklace hangs loosely around her slender neck.

Maybe Mother is wondering, as she looks directly into the camera, what is she doing? Wondering if her life is her own or something manufactured, and yet she doesn't imagine it going wrong, or whether her happiness is dependent on love or geography, circumstances of birth, the weather. Maybe she's not wondering about any of this, just going through the To-Dos in her mind: photos, cake, dancing, married life, family life inside the tight-knit Jewish community of Tulsa, followed by all those Shabbat dinners to come at my grandparents' house on East 38th Street. White tablecloth. Clean china. Brisket pulled from the oven. Maybe she's simply wondering, as she loops her left arm around my father's white-sleeved arm, should she hold his hand?

Twenty-seven years old, with short black hair, bright-eyed, a naval reservist, my father is pressed into a white tuxedo, a crooked boutonniere in his lapel. With two fingers he's squeezing a jacket button, his lean wrist extended past a thick cuff. He appears unafraid of life becoming hateful. His world not spinning on What Ifs. But is the look in his eyes a look of worry? Is he thinking he can't make enough money? Hates his job? But what else can he find?

My mother widens her eyes, and my father stiffens, when

they abandon themselves into fixed expressions. The pose is of long smiles, captured lost thoughts, smooth and secretive and silver and soft as cream when the cameraman presses the button to click open the shutter. The flash bursts like a life in the bulb.

I know these are normal enough troubles. No one was eaten by a bear. Nor was anyone killed in a train derailment. The story of my parents' marriage and divorce doesn't amount to a story of extremes, madness, or murder. Nothing like that. It's a portrait of a slow burn inside the historical predicament into which I was born. Little else about it needs to be said, except that by 1978, when I turned fourteen and they lived apart, my two older brothers had also moved away from home. Living alongside my mother in the house on Loch Lomond as the last son—while my father lived about a half mile west along the bayou—was like being the artificial leg of the family, something propped up when not in use, and just as familiar. Everyone seemed to feel sorry for me being the last kid in that house, even as I refused to feel sorry for myself.

I liked living in two minds: aware of the changes to my life and pressing on all the same. My affections and afflictions were my own. Overpowered by her new circumstance, Mother only tried to guess what I might be thinking—as I was about to pass by her from the dining room to the kitchen, or from the kitchen to the den, or back again, whichever room I was going to, to avoid talking or bumping into her.

T hose years in Texas felt like exile for my mother.

She didn't like the climate, she didn't like the atmosphere, and she was forever grieving for her family and friends in Tulsa. She spoke of being wronged, never mistaken. Wronged can't be remedied. Time alone she spent in her room reading, though it seemed she never had a day off. Days and nights came and went. We got into our beds and fell asleep and woke up.

The way things had been, a family of five, and the way things became, the two of us dodging each other inside the empty house on Loch Lomond, dredged a chasm between eras that could never be forded.

My mother believed it was her responsibility to raise Jewish sons, a duty she saw as set against adverse conditions. I understood her position to be that the vast air of gentile life hovered over the freeways and strip malls and churches of Texas and surrounded us inside Meyerland, until sooner or later the air settled above the waters of the bayous, or atop the flat buildings of the neighborhood's public schools, or seeped into the cracks of the sidewalks to emerge as crucified sprigs of grass.

Had my mother been a stone, she'd have been a stone of testimony to what has always been Jewish, and what will always be Jewish. A stone of days. A stone of the end of days. Nothing would cause her determination to succumb. From her, you would not be asked to consider the human spirit, but only the Jewish spirit. Not human aspiration, but Jewish aspiration. The thought frightened me. Curiosity made me feel I was always thinking wrongly, or perhaps I was sick. The old accusation, extermination by assimilation.

During the years of their marriage, my father, who was raised in a Jewish house in Oklahoma, but not a Jewish home, merely went along, hardly an accomplice. He felt little obligation to Judaism and assented to Mother's expectations around the rituals and calendar of Jewish experience. A navy diver for two tours in the Korean War, he donned his whites once a month for reserve duty and kept a sleek .22 in his sock drawer, though I never once saw him fire much less clean it. His sole Jewish act seemed to be membership in the Jewish Community Center's men's health club, where he repaired afternoons to play racquetball and jog and take a shower in one of the brown-tiled shower stalls with pump bottles of shampoo tipped precariously atop the aluminum safety railings, and where some days when I was in grade school I'd sneak in past a doctor's office scale that never wavered near a row of toilets and find him toweling off next to a damp wooden bench, where you'd have to push aside a scattering of men's socks and underwear to sit down.

So the dictates of Jewish life fell to my mother. It was like a dread that stabbed at her, something like indigestion, as if she believed she would never get another chance to correct your grievous ways. She was convinced that everything you might have done in the past or in the future consisted of abysmal conduct, some error, certainly discredit. My attending the Day School at Beth Yeshurun was Mother's idea. It was a small, distinguished school where we studied in Hebrew and learned Jewish culture. The Day School was known for producing disciplined, inquisitive students who were meant to develop moral integrity and become proficiently knowledgeable about prayer, Israel, and the Jewish people, and also be able to read, write, and speak Hebrew fluently. Fourteen years I attended the Day School, as well as junior high and senior high Talmud classes.

A great victory for my mother, the inheritor of the four matriarchs of the Jewish nation, came one Sunday morning in springtime when I was eleven. With all the bright leaves greenly splayed on Loch Lomond, I'd walked into the house from Lloyd Hartsfield's across the street, after his family was returning from their nearby church, and Lloyd said he couldn't play football in the yard.

Mother was resting on the sofa in the den with a novel on her lap.

What is Easter anyway? I said, and she held my two hands and thanked me, such that this question would be held high in her heart as an achievement for American Jewry, a win for a dark-eyed girl with the immigrant father, the one who closed up his scrap yard unusual days of the year with a sign on the gate, CLOSED FOR JEWISH HOLIDAY.

Recently my mother phoned with a beautiful, unusual offer.

She's in her eighties now, lives in Missouri, retired, and is still unillusioned, vehement, a woman of strictures, who is often left from society's heinous mores feeling flabbergasted.

—I want you to think about something. I'd like to buy a burial plot for you at the cemetery in Tulsa, where my father and mother are buried, and where I'm to be buried, she said over the telephone.

—You're going to outlive us all, I said and sat in a chair in my kitchen in Portland because I knew the offer was preamble to a soliloquy.

—I should have died a long time ago. It would have put me out of my misery.

This led to a recounting of my grandfather buying burial plots for my mother and her three sisters when she, my mother, was about my age.

—Think about it. It's your choice, she says, emphasizing the word *your*, and I was trying to remember what the rhetorical term is for saying one thing and meaning the opposite.

I had the feeling that the discussion about my future grave, where I would be buried for all eternity, meant I would never get these twenty minutes of my life back.

—My sister Marcia isn't buried in our section of the cemetery. She told Daddy she wanted to be buried in the temple section, not the synagogue section, to be with Uncle Jan when he dies. Well, Marcia, if that's your decision, Daddy said, you can come visit us when you're dead.

—Well I'll get back to you on that, I said, remembering something Kafka once wrote, "The meaning of life is that it stops."

All the while I was thinking, why are you offering just me a burial plot? What about Wendy? And the kids between us? What am I going to do? Get on an airplane after I die to be buried in Tulsa? C'mon, Tulsa? I live in Oregon. Anyway. I'm a Texan.

But what kind of Texan?

A Texan who lives in the Pacific Northwest. A Texan who loves the tintinnabulations of his Old Portland craftsman, built in 1915, situated on the east side of the Willamette River, with hundred-foot high fir trees and a smooth pond in Laurelhurst Park right across our busy street. A Texan who loves the sounds of the doors opening and closing, footsteps in the foyer, dogs barking against the windows, traffic outside in the road, garbled voices from a neighbor's stoop, shouts from living room to kitchen, dishwasher coughing, a knife chopping against a wooden cutting board, and, on a summer's night in the warm light of late evening, the scratchy radio broadcast of a ballgame.

I'm also a Texan who loves this home's silences. The empty rocking chair in the kitchen and another on the front porch worn by the wind. Books I've kept for three dozen years, all of them closed, on the long shelves of the library. Last week's mail stacked on a counter in the kitchen, with official-looking return addresses, that has yet to be opened. Dining room windows in their sashes. Dust in the corners of the hardwood floors.

If home is where we belong, and from where we depart, then perhaps the most difficult thing about assessing the causes of my exile from Texas is watching the events order themselves back into place. It's like setting up a canvas on which to make a portrait. First you steady the tripod and the tray of paints and brushes. You stand in front of the blank canvas and turn your head to observe the model, but it feels like you're the one who is naked. You mix the paints and start brushing on the paint. But what you're painting isn't what you're seeing. Or remembering. There's the motionless body of the model. Smooth skin. High cheeks. Rumble of thighs. But trying to look closely it's like you have no knowledge of the human body. None at all. Like you've never seen a human body. Or have no memory of seeing one.

Is that what it means to try to define your past?

What I see, when I think of Texas, is the scraggy footpath

alongside Brays Bayou, and flag poles with American, Texas, and Israeli flags bleaching in the sun.

What I see, when I think of Texas, is Hebrew graffiti on the walls of Meyerland Plaza, faces in the stores and playgrounds the faces of the Pale of Settlement. In the markets and in the restaurants, the checkout clerks and waiters and the cooks, all Jews. Jews in every public school.

What I see, when I think of Texas, from early morning until the evening dusk, are crowds of Jews coming and going, howling and laughing and wailing in the Jewish air. Jewish cars driven on Jewish roads. Jewish sidewalks, where Jews walk to and from shul, milling around under the blaze of the scorching sun.

Leaving Texas has always felt like my Exodus from that place of Exodus, a long and perilous journey away from Jewish existence, where I sought to become redeemed.

And yet, that metaphor troubles me, because the biblical Exodus seems less about an individual life than about God. The star of the story isn't Moses or the Hebrews, it's Yahweh. Yahweh is the superstar of the Exodus myth. Moses is in a supporting role. The Hebrews are the extras. The conflict of Exodus isn't how to sanctify oneself through relinquishment or disavowal. It isn't offered as a threshold experience or a pilgrimage. It's a story that gives you a portrait of God. There are a lot of Hebrew slaves, of course. They cry. They shriek. But God sees, and God knows, and God understands, and God does all the talking. God orders Moses to administer the plagues, kill children and destroy families, and inspire the Hebrews to pack up and leave Egypt. The Hebrews are merely witnesses to what God says and does. God's actions change the world, not human piety or penance. Even in the promise of the covenant between God and the Jews, in which God reaffirms his pledge to Abraham but also swears commitment to the Hebrews wandering in the wilderness, God is asserting God's bond.

I hear the objection. Look, God not only promised, but God delivered.

Here, again, it's God's story. God snatches the Hebrews from danger, defeats the forces of despair, and demands purity and discipline. God promises, God delivers. It's like a business motto: Service Not Excuses.

The working hypothesis is that people would have no moral compass if we were not somehow in thrall to an immutable God. You've got to give up a lot of self-respect to come to that conclusion. But that's just how the writers of the Torah fashioned it. People are weak. God is strong. One won't do the right thing or abstain from the wrong one except for the dream of a sacred reward or the dread of supernatural retribution.

How easily I can conjure that old animus.

Because even now, still, all these years later, I have more than once in my time woken up feeling feeble and nauseous like I was in some Jacob-and-the-Angel sweat.

Nothing prepares me for those rain-meshed mornings in Portland, in wintertime, when I come into consciousness feeling as if I were shackled to my own existence. The whole ark of my lungs feels hollowed out. My breaths so furrowed what remains in my chest is like dry dirt. Against the side of my windpipe my pulse is beating much too fast. To move my body from one side or the other in bed, faintly hearing myself breathe, is difficult. To shift from stomach to back, or the other way, trying not to wake Wendy, who is sleeping lightly beside me, as if under the spell of the incense of her Catholic dreams, or deeper, her Cherokee dreams, is a terror.

For an hour I lie still, trying not to alarm the dogs sleeping on the floor. The time feels compacted and dense. Slowly I adjust my eyes to the gray sky in the windows, the silhouette of brooding fir trees, so that my birth, as much as my death, begins to feel distant and bland. All that tension requires forethought and calculation. It takes a strenuous effort to sit up and place my feet on the floor, to cross the room to the bathroom, inside which I don't bother to turn on the light, but can see the contours of my face and disheveled hair as a shadow in the mirror. In the reflection is a fleeting dispatch, sometimes gentle, other times stark, throwing itself across my eyes.

With little effort, as my skin cools, and my face appears in the glass as if it were submerged in green water, I'm bewildered enough to think I'm standing under the hot sticky air of Texas, with chittering insects, and heavy clouds slumping over the landscape to wherever they're headed, like a circus closing up and moving on.

All of that abruptly sinks in my skin. The nodes of the past seem, in my blurry reflection in the mirror, big enough to be seen and felt. What's palpable moves from the inside out, a brusque truth, where no biopsy is needed.

What I see is, home.

It's in there, all right, the place that possesses the old faith, like a disagreeable angel.

But when I look in the mirror, I see what looks like a stranger who cuts off my tongue, and I stand dumbly staring as if I were under medical inspection, like I am sitting upright on a doctor's paper-trimmed table, the flashlight shrinking the pupils in my eyes, the doctor holding up a card with my name on it and asking, Can you read that? Other mornings, I feel like I'm almost trotting, my thoughts appearing and disappearing as if growing out of the ground. Swish of cars in pairs shooting ahead on the long streets, appearing to go nowhere. Above the telephone lines are loose threads of clouds. A matted blue sky.

I strike up a silent conversation.

The stranger in the mirror speaks first. A thick Texas drawl.

—Look who it is. Is it really you? After all this time? Passing through? he asks, staring the way people do when they can see just fine but want to convey mystery.

—You know, here and there, I say.

—Well, living is trouble. See? *Le-koot cha-mal chut-kahl ola-mim Um-ehm hahl-te-cha, Be-kahl dor vah-dor,* he says in a whisper.

I make no expression and focus on the new gray hair above my ears.

— You've forgotten? You've forgotten?

— Your kingdom is forever in all worlds, and from generation to generation passes your dominion, I say and study the scar on my nose that bends like a creek on a small hill.

I blink the image in the mirror away, and shudder, like a dog shaking water from its fur, and turn on the overhead light to return, well, to what exactly?

My understanding of my home where I live now, in Portland, is something I try to forge inside the life I live. But I also feel the forging. I know that this home is being made from the slippage of earlier ones. "Memory is not an instrument for exploring the past but its theater," writes Walter Benjamin, adding "it is the medium of past experience, as the ground is the medium in which dead cities lie interred."

I thought of this idea recently because Wendy has been sending me online links about the inexpensive cost of living in Kiev, thinking we might consider retiring there.

Yes, that Kiev.

I say to her, my people didn't flee the shtetls of Ukraine, dodging Bolsheviks and Poles and Cossacks, so that, after a hundred years in America, their offspring, free as any Jews in the world, would up and go back. Oy, I say to her with a comic air, you wouldn't believe, not three days after we moved to Kiev, again with the pogroms.

But the question persists.

What is the point of making a new home, if not to be alert to the mystery of its presence in relation to the spirit of all those homes that preceded it?

One of those mysteries is a Friday night, in May, 1976, when I was twelve, while my father was still in St. Luke's Hospital on Holcombe Boulevard two months after his stroke, when my mother gave my brothers and me the report of the latest round of his Porch Index aphasia assessment test.

That was the year I was learning that some things in life are irrevocable.

It was past sundown by the time we gathered for Shabbat at the dining room table. Roasted chicken, baked potato, string beans with mushrooms, and buttery green peas. A warmed round challah ordered from Three Brothers Bakery near Stella Link Road.

We're all standing around the table, awaiting Mother's recitation of the prayer over the Shabbat candles, followed by the chanting of the Kiddush over the Shabbat wine, when she announces the test results. For communication abilities, where a normal score is 15.0, and the minimum normal for aphasiacs is 10.0, she says, your father scored 8.0 overall. The normal score for gestural skills on the test is 15.0 with a minimum of 12.0 for aphasiacs. Your father's gestural score was 10.5. Worst was his verbal score, she says. The normal score on the Porch Index is 15.0.

— What'd he get? I ask.

— The minimum is 10.0 for aphasiacs. Your father scored 4.8.

— Yesterday he was saying some words, Matt says, sixteen that year, and he's tapping his hands on the back of his chair where he was standing.

— Come on, we don't have to talk about the tests, Scott says.

My brothers are standing at opposite sides of the dining room table that's covered with a white cloth and white dishes. The two of them had long since succumbed to being unfriendly toward each other, as if each had a private disinterest in the other's existence, wholly free of guilt or obscure details of camaraderie. All the friendly-looking photographs of them to-gether when they were small, before I was born—attired with crisp clothes for a first day of school, in matching coat and tie for High Holidays, Halloween get-ups—merely hid that Scott, the older by a year, could not abide the birth of the other. And Matt, who possessed the ability to stay quiet for long stretches, as if he was awake and dreaming at the same time, wasn't tak-ing any of his guff.

—Going to get better whether they test him or not, I say.

—What's wrong with you? He may never get better, says Scott.

—Leave him alone, Matt says, and Scott lurches forward like he's going to shove Matt in the chest.

—The three of you, stop it, Mother scolds us all and waves her palms in the air over two white candle sticks as if to start a spell to kindle the soul of every person in the house with God's lamp, then covering her eyes, and saying the Hebrew prayer to praise God for providing a path to holiness. Twin flames reflect in the windows, emanating into the room.

Staring at the white table cloth and cutlery, I lift my Kiddush cup of sweetened red wine, twirling it in my fingertips so the liquid sloshes at the edges, and I chant from heart the long ver-sion of the Kiddush in Hebrew, the taut words scratched out of my mouth to prescribe the gift of rest, a completion of God's creation past every door and into every corner of the house, flashing the ancient codes of those words with the filters of their meanings, like faint names whispered over the skin of the night.

The Fifth Child

Hardly had Mrs. Rothman let us in the front door on Rice Avenue with *Chag Sameach, Y'all's*, all around, than she hustled back to the kitchen in her plaid dress. Her parents, the Bernsteins, had driven from Nebraska, as they did every year, and Mr. Bernstein was making horseradish near the pantry. With my father and brothers we arrived in coats and ties and were whisked into the living room where the Rothman sisters, Marcy and Andrea, in trim dresses, were sitting on the sofa fielding questions about school from Mother, who'd been sent out of the kitchen from where all afternoon she'd been helping with preparations.

Mother took pains to avoid Scott, fifteen that year, who reeked of pot, in order to approach me and cinch my tie. Matt, fourteen, found a spot on the carpeted floor, spread his legs in a wide V, while thumbing through a back issue of *Time* magazine that had Soviet dissident Alexander Solzhenitsyn's tawny-maned face on the cover. The Rothman sisters—Marcy, a year older than me, Andrea, a year younger—were talking to Mother in a friendly tone. There was sharp fussing between Mrs. Rothman and her father in the kitchen. Followed by flurries of Yiddish.

The year was 1974.

It was the beginning of a long affair, the Rothman's annual Passover Seder. Attending were the five of us, my grandparents who hadn't yet arrived from their hotel near the Galleria on Westheimer Road, the four Rothmans, and their two grandparents. Later Moie Hamburger, an old friend of the Bernsteins, was sure to burst in. The Rothman's Seder, for years and years, had gone off easily, paced by the rhythms of the Maxwell House Haggadah. Dr. Rothman, a professor of British literature at the University of Houston, ran the evening like a seminar on Samuel Johnson's *The History of Rasselas, Prince of Abyssinia*. Everyone was expected to read aloud and then, especially the children, to be called upon to field questions about their portion without fussiness. Discussion, jokes, old tales, all of it modeled, including the wine, on a Platonic symposium.

That night, long after six o'clock, there was no sign of sitting down for the Seder yet. Some worry was expressed Moie might arrive stewed and be hard to manage. Scott had said he would take the job of dealing with Moie this year—when I looked at him to be sure what he meant, he raised his hand to his mouth, squeezed together thumb and forefinger, tapped his lips twice with a gleeful menace and inhaled with two quick bursts like he was toking a joint. Moie's arrival was hard to predict, but we all wondered what was keeping my grandparents. To peer out a window of the ranch house, Mother kept walking toward the front windows into Dr. Rothman's open study, the shelves lined with anthologies, commentaries, criticism, collections of poetry, short stories, and novels, and resting on top of an open dictionary his gold-fringed purple tallit bag with a gold Star of David in the center. Rice Avenue ran one way on this side of the bayou, and it took a knowing maneuver to get to the Rothman's curb. Rice is such a difficult street to navigate, Mother said out loud more or less to nobody, while peering through the flat curtains.

They're here! called Mrs. Rothman when she opened the door, followed by hugs, shaking of hands, expressions of worry, and kisses near powdered cheeks. My grandfather joked about how long it takes his wife to get ready and praised her appearance. With a half-unamused look, my grandmother smiled at everyone and glanced around—she appeared small in the dim light of the foyer, with a pale complexion, and melon-colored hair.

— Everyone has trouble with our one way street. But you're here! *Chag Sameach*! *Chag Sameach*! They're here! Mrs. Rothman called out and hustled back into the kitchen.

Mother and Mrs. Rothman had met as girls at Jewish summer camp in the 1940s. The sets of grandparents had known each other through the webbed world of little Jewish communities across dozens of Midwestern towns. Names were dropped like old crumbs. Salutations offered from mutual acquaintances. All of us children had stood and were greeted formally, laughing vigorously. Kisses. *Chag Sameach*! *Chag Sameach*! A warm air from the stove coupled with the spring humidity stiffened in the living room and escaped into the dining room where, before long, we were gathered and standing behind our assigned, high-backed seats. I looked down at the floor, at the slender legs on the chairs, pairs of feet, and listened to Dr. Rothman, at the head of the table, open the Seder. We are about to begin the recitation of the ancient story of Israel's redemption from bondage in Egypt, he said, and he read from the Haggadah that the purpose of this Seder is to afford us the opportunity to recall the dramatic and miraculous events which led to the Exodus from an ancient land of slavery.

Dr. Rothman brought forward a stout, professorial bearing, right up to his high forehead, thin hair, and black yarmulke. His eyeglasses, perched close on his face, reflected the Haggadah. His goatee was trimmed for the occasion. We stood for a few moments shuffling our feet, while the place settings waited on the table to be clacked.

I took a look at all the mothers, each keenly dressed in a neat skirt and hair trimmed to a shine. Not one mother gave a look of being in an unfamiliar place but stood erect, confident. Seder nights had long ago been braided into the color of their lives. Once we sat down we commenced to read the Haggadah, one person after another clockwise around the table. After each portion someone nodded appreciatively or patted the reader reassuringly, and a hearty murmur erupted, followed by side comments, a raised eyebrow, a quip, a smart-aleck reply. By and by an efficiency took hold. Reader after reader recited passages from the Haggadah, and that was followed by a nodding of heads slowly as we told the story of the Israelites escape from bondage. Some read with a knitted brow. Some read slightly charged. Scott read with contempt and Andrea read with glee and I read with solemnity and Marcy read with brisk tact and Matt read with anxious testimony. The adults read with tones running from patronizing to patriotic.

Soon Matt's mood grew irritated. He began pointing out how inefficient the Egyptian political machine, he called it, was for trying to kill the male Jewish children by casting them into the Nile. Whose idea was it that after Pharaoh couldn't—he paused to find the words in the Haggadah—"subdue them with forced labor" to then round them up, drive them down to the river where everyone could see the children forced underwater?

Mother at first appreciated his interest, then a shadow passed over her look.

—Do you have an observation about this passage? Dr. Rothman asked Matt with encouragement.

Matt nodded and took a breath. Scott, who usually led the resistance at Seder, leaned back and rested his hands behind his neck. The two of them lined up in size and build that year. Where Scott's face was fleshy, and Matt's narrowed, both had wide noses and long hair that covered their foreheads and collars. Scott had already been rubbing his neck and scraped a small red spot, like a blush of blood, as if whatever turmoil was troubling him was clawing at his throat. Matt spoke about how the whole procedure made no sense, that it would have been easy to resist, to overwhelm—checking the Haggadah— the "task masters." Everyone would have seen it, he argued. He was going through his prosecution the way you pick up an object at a second hand store and turn it over in your hand. He was interested in it, but not enough to buy it. He wrapped up

his point quickly and expected the responsive readings to go
on, first smiling, then making an inattentive face.

—You should be quite ashamed of yourself, Matthew.
Tonight is not the time, Mother said.

—Of course it is. Tonight of all nights we are together
again and at ease with the immensity of our freedom, said Mr.
Bernstein.

—Saved your ass, Scott whispered.

—This part also shows how just God is, Marcy said with a
warm drawl.

—And merciful, Mrs. Bernstein said.

—And merciful. But to the Israelites, Grandma Selma, not
to the Egyptians. Because when God instructs the Hebrews to
take a lamb and kill it and put the blood on the door of the
house and stay inside the house until morning while the angel
of death passes over all the houses, God is allowing anyone to
choose to obey or not. We've been talking about this at school
when Rabbi Segal came to our class. It's a question of justice
and trust, he told us. And we know that God will keep his
word. It was the Egyptians who had killed the Hebrew children and threw them into the Nile. Now it was their turn to
feel the pain of losing a child.

Dr. Rothman winked at Marcy and spoke of the importance
of Matt's questions, before pressing behind our chairs to perform one of the Seder's symbolic acts of purification, the ritual
of washing his hands. There was talk of which of us was attending classes at the shul for Junior Congregation or Shabbos on
Sunday, Tallis N' Tefillin or Hillel High, in addition to those of
us still young enough to attend the Day School.

—Your mother tells me you're thinking of going to the
University of Texas, Scott, said Mrs. Bernstein.

—No, I plan to go right to work in the garbage business.

I watched my parents, who were seated separately, react
separately.

—Don't get me started, Mother said with a frown and
looked at my father who rolled his eyes and patted the denim

yarmulke tighter onto his head, then rubbed his fingertips along the top of the table's edge, before gazing up at the ceiling as if he alone could hear some distant tune, and the music was sweeping against the roof of the house and drifting toward the city's glassy skyline.

—Well, son, hold on there, think about it, my grandfather said.

—You didn't go to college, Scott said.

—There was the Depression.

—Deciding about this can wait, said my grandmother, and she touched Scott on the elbow as easily as she might have been putting down a spoon.

Mr. Bernstein kept leaning back in his seat and twisting his head so he could look out the window for Moie Hamburger.

—What are you looking for, Grandpa Nate, Andrea asked, and switched her soup spoon with her dessert spoon and back again.

One of the occasions in Meyerland that made the place seem so insular to someone growing up Jewish there was Rabbi Segal's annual reenactment of the biblical Exodus.

Earlier that day of the Seder at the Rothman's, that spring of 1974, my father agreed to accompany me on the rabbi's Exodus, having said previously I wasn't sure I would go, and for days Mother kept saying how much fun it would be with my friends.

Dozens of children and a handful of adults, upwards to a hundred people or more, gathered in the parking lot of Beth Yeshurun early in the morning to start the three mile hike to the Jewish Community Center along the sloping embankment of Brays Bayou, our Red Sea for the day. It was several months since Egypt and Israel had signed a disengagement accord after the Yom Kippur War. Israel withdrew from the western bank of the Suez Canal, while Egypt agreed to a troop reduction and a United Nations-patrolled buffer zone. In Meyerland that spring, armed guards were still stationed at all the synagogues's entrances. The rabbi made a point of the political situation when he joked that the Jews are still negotiating with the Egyptians the terms of the ancient departure.

A lean man with peppery hair, Rabbi Segal stood on top of the curb, impersonating Moses with his white tallit wrapped over his head like a keffiyeh. Those who saw him grew quiet. Some may have thought at first he was going to describe the route we were taking. Others could see he was ceremonially stretching his arm outward from beneath his white robe until people grew very quiet, tilted their eyes, lifted their heads, nodded, nodded again in a great rhythm, used their eyes to indicate to others to look at the rabbi as the morning light simmered above us. To stare upwards at his shadowed eyes was to meet the upper part of his face with its intellectual cast, small, smooth chin, long side burns. He smiled big and youthfully. He seemed incapable of offering an imposing countenance, but he could anger. You knew it when the wrinkles in his forehead tightened and his cheeks slackened.

The longer we watched, the more pleased he became. He stood utterly still, like a ship that had dropped anchor. He could be seen from every angle. None attempted to make sense of his presence. His body was a familiarity everyone knew. We didn't wait around to be told what was next. No novices among us, whispering, and quieting. But none wanted to miss the moment when the rabbi adjusted the keffiyeh and raised a long wooden shepherd's crook over his head.

—To the Promised Land! he called.

With hey-ohs and yeeehaws and move-em-outs the Houston branch of the children of Israel cascaded out of the parking lot as if on a cattle drive, turning toward Newcastle Street. We covered some of the same terrain as the Go Texan Day paraders from a few months earlier. When the Day School was released to watch the riders and covered wagons pass by the shul, announcing the beginning of rodeo season that kicked off every year with the Houston Livestock Show at the Astrodome, we all sat on the curb and watched the parade. Blonde cowgirls with black Stetsons rode high on brown and white horses, each hoisting a Texas flag. White boys with their blue jeans tucked into cowboy boots and donning silver cowboy hats marched by. Black high school cheerleaders danced in short white skirts and waved green and white pompoms. There were marching bands of every shape and size, clarinets and tubas shining against white-gloved hands in the sunlight. A single rider with a gold sombrero rode a tall tan horse and twirled a lasso. Military riders in service blues and white cowboy hats clicked at the sides of white horses. So many Lone Star flags. American flags. Confederate flags. A red-headed elderly woman hollered over and over, Let's Rodeo, Houston! More covered wagons. More marching bands, in bright slacks and trim jackets. Congressmen waved stetsons. Clowns danced with yellow and blue kerchiefs hanging from their belt buckles, and donning polka dot ties. Old-fashioned fire trucks. More lasso riders. More high school marching bands, clad in black, with white spats, and white feathered hats. Baton twirlers, so many you couldn't keep count, until they all faded in the distance under the horizon, and after the last float disappeared, like a brazen plume, we returned inside the shul.

In Meyerland, Jews mostly adopted the looks and accents of Texas. We spoke Hebrew with a southern accent, punctuated ironically with y'all. *Shalom, y'all. Boker Tov, y'all.* There were still people in the neighborhood in those days who were survivors of Nazi concentration camps. The imprint of Eastern European Jewry was heard through the use of Yiddish as tribal code: bubbe and bupkes, chutzpah, goy, kibbitz, mensch and mazel tov, schmuck, tchotchke, potchke, tuchus, shtup, shvitz, shiksa, schlep.

For sure, that Passover morning, our Exodus attire couldn't have been less Texan, decked out in puka shell necklaces and Birdwell beach britches, marching in our Tiddies sandals.

Children ran in all directions along the bayou, trailing behind the rabbi's robe. Like herders in the Sinai, parents took up the rear, their heads bent in conversation. No one pretended to imagine we were destined to some strip of desert along the Dead Sea. As none of those on the biblical Exodus could have imagined the American South of brick houses we trekked alongside of, not at all like the Judaean wilderness or Mount Carmel or the coast plains of Galilee, but a flat stretch of lowlands inside the Old Confederacy.

So many Texas towns and counties and geographical features, from the Guadalupe Mountains to Padre Island, derive their names from Catholic Spanish explorers and conquistadors beginning in the eighteenth century, that it can be surprising to learn that Samuel Isaacks, one of the earliest Jewish settlers, had settled near the Brazos River in 1821. Or that Adolphus Sterne, an Orthodox Jew, slaveholder, and Justice of the Peace, who arrived in Texas in 1826, helped finance the Texas Revolution. By 1838 Jews were living in Bolivar, Galveston, Nacogdoches, San Antonio, and Velasco. With them came the development of Jewish institutions, the building of Jewish cemeteries, the first of which, in 1852, was plotted in Galveston. By the turn of the twentieth century, synagogues could be found throughout the state, in Houston, San Antonio, Dallas, Austin, Waco, Gainesville, and Marshall, in Texarkana, in Corsica, in Tyler, and elsewhere.

Of all the early rabbis to serve in Texas, Henry Cohen of Galveston's B'nai Israel left the greatest legacy, serving for six decades beginning in 1888. From 1907 to 1914, the Galveston Movement, spearheaded by Rabbi Cohen, settled some ten thousand Jewish immigrants through Texas. Galveston was a passenger port for the North German Lloyd shipping company, based in the German port of Bremen, through which East European Jews traditionally left the continent, including my mother's family from Ukraine. Between 1900 and 1920 estimates of the Jewish population in Dallas, Fort Worth, Houston, and San Antonio grew from fifteen thousand to thirty thousand.

Sixteen-year-old Joseph Francis Meyer, a German Protestant Catholic, had settled in Houston following the Civil War when, after the sudden death of his father, he started a wagon-materials business and hardware store in downtown Houston. He was an alderman, chief of the fire department, prominently identified with the Houston National Bank, and a major figure in the Texas Democratic Party. Little more is known of Joseph Francis Meyer except that he began buying up six thousand acres of land, mostly rice farms, in the southwest edge of the city on the correct assumption that Houston would spread in that direction. The conversion of these abandoned rice fields into an eventual two thousand–home subdivision under the supervision of George Meyer, one of Joseph's sons, was greeted, in 1955, with a ribbon-cutting ceremony at what would become the open air courtyard of Meyerland Plaza, by Vice President Richard Nixon, who brought a message from Washington, DC, about how Meyerland was making it possible for America to lead the world to peace and to provide hope for peoples on both sides of the Iron Curtain, for freedom and for justice.

The story of how the Jews came to Meyerland, in the middle of the twentieth century, begins in River Oaks, Houston's wealthy garden community that emerged around the River Oaks Country Club in the 1920s. The club hosted the annual Old South Plantation Ball, complete with elaborate period costumes and carriage rides, an event that brought the most prominent families in Texas, including former governors and congressmen. Money raised went to the Old South Plantation Confederate Museum.

In the 1920s, as mansions were erected in River Oaks and whites moved in, wealthy Jews, Hispanics, and African-Americans looking to buy a house equal to their economic status would arrive at a showing to find the promised lock box missing, or the key you picked up at the real estate office didn't work. The house you were interested in was just sold, you were told, even though it remained on the market for a year. Real estate agents who, if they had even returned your phone call, agreed to meet you at houses to open them didn't show. Or they'd suggest you'd be happier living elsewhere in the city, in West University, or Riverside Terrace.

Throughout the 1930s and 1940s, wealthy Jewish families built original-designed Art Deco homes in Riverside Terrace. Families like the Battlesteins, the Fingers, the Sakowitzes, and the Weingartens hired renowned architects to build estates meant to rival the houses of River Oaks and other wealthy neighborhoods. They built in front of the alleyways and bridges that crisscross the small ditches that feed into the city's bayous. Soon Riverside became an integrated neighborhood of middle class Jews and white Christians, the neighborhood for Houston's synagogues as well as a small Jewish Community Center. By the end of the Second World War there were some fifteen thousand Jews living in Houston, many in Riverside Terrace, the so-called Jewish River Oaks.

In Meyerland, the future neighborhood for Houston's Jews, new housing starts began in 1952, the same year everything in Riverside started to change. That was the year wealthy African-American cattle rancher Jack Caesar began looking for a mansion in Houston for his young family. As Caesar searched the real estate listings, he found his options limited throughout segregated Houston, until he found a brick estate he liked in Riverside Terrace, and gave his white male secretary money to purchase the house. Afterward, Caesar's secretary transferred the deed, and the Caesar family moved into their new home in the middle of the night.

The first year, there existed little tension between the Caesar household and their white Christian and Jewish neighbors. Then, in April 1953, four sticks of dynamite exploded on the Caesar's front porch. The windows shattered. Lathe and plaster blew in every direction. There was yelling. Sirens. Spotlights from police cars. It took days to sweep up all the tinkling bits of glass from the street. Had the Caesar family been home, perhaps asleep, when the bomb exploded, the blast might have lifted them from their beds.

Soon after the explosion, whites and Jews started to move out of the neighborhood. Some even used the River Oaks model, one must call it, and encouraged those moving out of Riverside Terrace to agree not to sell their homes to blacks. In 1959, seven years after the Caesars moved in—and as other African American families bought homes in Riverside, and home prices for a time plunged, and white residents were leaving the neighborhood—city planners and the Texas Department of Transportation took a fresh look at the alignment for what would be State Highway 288 and decided to put the route of the planned freeway through the east end of Riverside Terrace. The path of the new eight-lane highway would cut right through Jack Caesar's home.

By the 1970s almost all the palatial homes in Riverside were owned by African Americans, and the neighborhood would go on to become to the city's black community what it had once been to the Jewish community, a new haven for middle class life.

Now Houston's Jews, joining the wave of white flight, had migrated to the southwest side of the city across Brays Bayou. With the relocation and construction of a new Beth Yeshurun Synagogue and Day School on Beechnut Street in 1962 and a new Temple Beth Israel on North Braeswood in 1967, Meyerland became my family's home when we arrived in our blue Oldsmobile station wagon in 1968. First we found a one-story brick house with a shady willow tree on Lymbar Drive near Johnston Junior High School. Soon after we moved to Loch Lomond to be closer to the new Jewish Community Center which was built in 1969.

That year, Houston's population was 1.2 million. The Jewish population had risen to twenty thousand. Most lived in Meyerland.

In a grassy opening at the intersection of Rice and Braeswood, Rabbi Segal stopped to deliver his Exodus sermon. Rubberneckers in passing cars slowed to observe the gathering, followed by a sprinkling of honks. The horizon rested in the distance like a thin sheet. Families that hadn't brought water murmured about the hot walk, and I imagined some murmured against God as the Israelites had with their ingratitude toward Moses, their slander and rebellions alongside encounters with strangers who refused to accept God's commandments, and the necessity to avoid towns that wouldn't let the Hebrews pass through. If only the rabbi could dip his staff into the muddy bayou, as Moses did into the little streams in the desert after he snapped off a piece of a laurel tree and wrote God's name on it and threw it in the water, whereupon it became drinkable and sweet.

With sweat on his face the rabbi told the story of the biblical Exodus now that we were, he said, halfway to the Promised Land, indicating the distance from where we had stopped to the Jewish Community Center up ahead, still out of view. A slow silence came over us all. The smallest children wandered without restraint and kicked at the dust. Rabbi Segal spoke in the first person as if he had personally been with the Hebrews who rushed to leave Egypt, and that he had personally received the Ten Commandments.

—When we lived in Egypt we were free. It was only after the death of Joseph did we notice a change toward us, the Jewish people. The Egyptians hated us. They envied us, and they feared us because we had multiplied into a great nation. The seventy people Joseph had brought into Egypt now numbered six-hundred thousand. Behold, one rapacious advisor to Pharaoh said, the people of the children of Israel are mighty. Let us destroy them before they become too numerous and join our enemies against us in war. So Pharaoh made a plan. He cunningly lured our Hebrew men to help him build up some of his cities by promising high wages, and then once we men arrived we were not paid but enslaved.

The rabbi cleared his throat to talk theatrically evil, like he was Edgar G. Robinson as Rico in *Little Caesar.*

—It will work, this plan, see. We'll build great cities, see. And the children of Israel will work to death. Who do you think they're talking to. One of us has got to lose, and it ain't gonna be me, see. I'm not taking any chance. We'll prevent them from being with their wives and making new families, see. I'll show 'em.

Scattered boos came from all the kids who had settled on the ground among the buzzing insects.

—But God heard the affliction of his people. He recalled his promise to Abraham that He would make his children as numerous as the stars in the heavens, the rabbi called out.

He's going to take forty years to tell this story, my father whispered after the rabbi had been talking for twenty minutes.

—All this talk of manna is making me hungry. We don't have manna from heaven. But the Men's Club is waiting at the Center with bagels and lox and cream cheese and coffee and juice. Manna from Alfred's Delicatessen. To the Promised Land! he cried out, and he raised his wooden staff above his head and called us to stand and wipe the dust from our clothing.

Uncomplaining, I walked on, skipping alongside the rabbi, and he began to talk to me about the last, laborious hours of Moses's life that we'd been learning about in school, when Moses cleaned Joshua's shoes and placed them beside the bed as Joshua slept, when he cleaned Joshua's cloak and turban, polished Joshua's helmet, and laid them all back in place on a golden chair.

—On the day he was to die, Moses wrote thirteen scrolls of the Torah, twelve for the twelve tribes, and one extra he set inside the Holy Ark to remain untouched so no one could falsify the Torah. And then God held the sun in place, saying, I will not set the sun, so long as Moses lives. Did you know that? said the rabbi.

—Is that when God pointed to the Promised Land and said

to Moses, This is the land which I swore unto Abraham, unto Isaac, and unto Jacob?

—Saying, I will give it to your seed. Yes. Well done. To them did I promise, but to you I show it, God said. Thing is, Moses fought off death until he was assured by God that his soul would walk in the land of the living.

—Why can't Moses go into Israel? I said.

—Right? Why is that? Because he's just across the river Jordan, and you'll remember that river is like the one between Jacob and Esau, the Jabbok River, when Jacob fights with the angel. There are always choices. Right? This side of the river. And?

—That side of the river.

—Always a divide.

—I don't understand why Moses thinks God is preventing him from going to the Promised Land then. He's old. He's dying. Least he could do for Moses, after all that time. And, why does he have to serve Joshua? Can't he just die in peace?

—Have you had anyone close to you die? A cat? A dog?

—We have a dog, a boxer. She's nine. Her legs are bad. But that's because she chases cars and barks at them and gets caught up in their tires.

—That's scary.

—She's a good dog, otherwise.

—Well Moses is trying to demonstrate to Joshua that the old must step aside for the young. When I talk to you and I hear you ask such good questions, I'm as proud of that as I would be of my own thinking. You see? I want you to ask questions. See? So that you can, what?

—Cross the river.

—Correct.

The rabbi moved closer, nodding, but not saying anything, and he extended a soft hand as if he saw something pulsating in me. I shook it, and we locked eyes. We shook our hands up and down, held still, up and down again, like you see when heads of state shake hands. If you had seen us alongside the high-grassy slope of the bayou that hot spring morning, with Temple Beth Israel and the JCC up ahead and Beth Yeshurun behind us, you would not have expected we were anything but mentor and pupil. Our quarrel was seven years off. When it happened, it was as unexpected as it was inevitable.

D r. Rothman noted before him were three matzos wrapped in white linen.

—I now perform the ceremony of *Yachatz*. I shall break the middle matzoh in two, removing one half and setting it aside. This will become the afikomen, the dessert, to be eaten at the conclusion of the meal. It reminds us that, as dessert, the best of redemption is yet to come, hidden.

He looked mischievously at the youngest at the table, his daughter, Andrea.

—Hidden somewhere in this house, she said.

Cheers rumbled around the Seder table. Dr. Rothman snapped the flat cracker and wrapped one half in another cloth napkin. He slipped the afikomen next to his plate. The custom of hiding this piece of matzoh so children find it and return it for a gift was a highlight of the dinner.

Following the Four Questions sung by Andrea, someone offered a Fifth Question, How did so many Jews end up in this section of the city?

—God brought us here, Dr. Rothman said.

—God? Scott said, rubbing his neck and nodding at my father who adjusted his yarmulke and chuckled.

—You don't agree?

—Agree? You mean, God spoke to Moses and said to him, "I am the Lord. I appeared to Abraham, to Isaac, and to Jacob, as God Almighty. I established my covenant with them to give them the land of Meyerland?"

—*Eretz* Meyerland, I said, using the Hebrew word for land, and a cheer went up.

—Just like on today's Exodus across the bayou, called out Mrs. Rothman.

—Yes! That's right! This land, this *Eretz* Meyerland, in which we live as sojourners, and God said, "I have heard the groaning of the people of Israel whom the Egyptians hold as slaves, and I have remembered my covenant all the way to Harris County, in the shadow of the Astrodome," Dr. Rothman laughed, and he slapped the table so that the silverware clinked.

—Say, therefore, I am the Lord, and I will redeem you with an outstretched arm and with great acts of judgment, and with a swimming pool in every third house and racquetball courts at the JCC, Marcy said.

—I will be your God of pastrami and lox at Alfred's Deli, my father said.

—This land is your land, this land is Meyerland, my mother called out.

—You shall know that I am the Lord your God as you live alongside the great Brays Bayou, and I will take you to be my people to dine at Kaphans and Hickory BBQ, Andrea said.

—And, lo, all your *cha-noot* in Braeswood Square will be run by the children of Israel. Weingarten's Grocer, Gifts N Gab, Play Mart, Michael's Jewelry, Music Land, all owned by Jewish families, Mrs. Rothman said to applause, after which the fathers drained and refilled their glasses of wine.

We pressed on, deeper into the Haggadah, with the call and response of the Four Sons.

The rabbi had visited our classes a few days before, and he had spoken of the Wise Son as the one who follows the rules of the community, but the Wicked Son rebels against them, while the Simple Son follows the rules without understanding them, and the Last Son, who does not know how to ask, just waits for dinner.

—Which son are you, do you think? Dr. Rothman asked me.

—Wicked, I said, tongue in cheek.

—No, no, no. Are you? Wicked? I want to know, said Dr.

Rothman, and he cleared his throat.

My grandfather watched me closely. With his eyes he encouraged me to answer, and while others were talking around the room, he waved a hand at everyone to quiet. My grandmother stretched her arm behind grandfather's shoulders, as she sat, smiling, amused to watch the Socratic manner in which the Seder was being run.

—Actually I'm all of them, I said.

—Smart ass, Scott coughed out, shushed by the others.

—Ok. Go on. How is it possible you can be four sons in one? said Dr. Rothman.

—Well I want to be the wise one. I know about duty and obligations, rituals, the prayers. We learn them every year. I know how to do them and can do them easily. But sometimes I don't agree with it.

—Honestly, Mother said.

—It's okay. It's okay. Let him talk, my grandmother said, waving me on.

—That would make me wicked. Sometimes I just do what I'm told, and other times I just don't even get it. Or even need to get it. I mean, I just get it. I don't have any questions. I don't need any questions. So I don't have to ask anything. I'm all of them.

Marcy touched her temple with a three-fingered salute.

—He could be none of them. The wise child might be observant but not necessarily have any deep understanding of what he's doing. You're not that. The wicked child might not be naturally evil. Something terrible, some great pain, might have caused him to separate from everyone else and to rebel against everyone. Nothing like that has happened to you. He's not the simple son because if he were simple-minded he wouldn't have come up with that answer, she said.

—That's clever, Mrs. Rothman said, her voice rising.

—Same goes for the son who doesn't know enough to ask. To say you could be all four and not feel you have to pick one means you know too much already. So you could be none of them, she said, steadied by her logic, and turning to some of the others to add a footnote I couldn't hear.

—Just don't become the fifth child, the one who is absent, who doesn't come to Seder, Mother said.

—We would never forget the lost son, Mrs. Rothman said and shook her head.

My grandfather had his elbows on the table and his fingers interlaced.

—You know, four is an important number. We drink four cups of wine. There are four questions. There are the four sons, he said.

My father talked about the four seasons and four elements and four directions on the compass. After Dr. Rothman spoke of the four corners of a building as the foundation of existence, Mr. Bernstein added that there are four tzitzit on the tallit, the fringes we hold to show how we are gathered from the four corners of the earth and that we touch to the parchment of the Torah scroll to show our love for our covenant with God.

Dr. Rothman said there are four character traits as well, according to *Pirkei Avot*, the compilation of Jewish ethical teachings. The starting point of character is how one divides up the world, he said. There is the average trait: What's mine is mine and yours is yours. There is the trait of the peasant: What's mine is yours and yours is mine. The trait of the saintly person: What's mine is yours and yours is yours. And the trait of the scoundrel: Yours is mine and mine is mine.

—*Pirkei Avot* also says there are four temperaments, my grandfather said and smiled, enjoying this seminar on Jewish thought.

—In my years as a professor, I've taught four types of students. Those who are quick to understand but quick to forget. Those who understand with difficulty but forget with difficulty. Those who are quick to understand and forget with difficulty. They are the wise ones. And those who understand with difficulty and are quick to forget. They are the unfortunate, Dr. Rothman said.

—We call those the strainer, the sifter, the sponge, and the funnel, Mrs. Rothman said to laughter and applause.

—There are four wives at this table, Andrea said, and the table cheered.

—And four mothers, like the four matriarchs, my mother said.

—There are four types who give tzedakah, my grandmother said of the moral obligation to give to charity, and after that we quieted.

—Any others? asked Dr. Rothman, resting his elbows near his plate and tapping together his opened palms.

There was a lot of nodding at the question, and shaking of heads. He had something in mind. He looked at me, and said my name.

—Four ways to understand Torah? I said.

—Exactly. Scott, can you name one of the ways to understand Torah?

—*Peshat*, the direct meaning, Scott said and scratched his neck.

Dr. Rothman pointed to Marcy

—*Drash*, interpretation, she said.

Then he pointed to Andrea and Matt in quick succession like he was shooting pistols.

—*Remez*, they said together.

—Yes, right, exactly. The deeper meaning of the interpretation.

—Well they are making Beth Yeshurun Day School proud, Mrs. Rothman cheered.

Finally he pointed to me to give the answer to the fourth way.

—*Sod*. God's meaning, I said and rested my elbows on the table.

—Not too shabby, Mr. Bernstein called out.

—Wonderful answers, Mrs. Bernstein said, and she clapped her hands.

Throughout the house, lined up in the many bookcases,

cosseted in large leather bindings with gold edges, dark-covered prayer books along with books on Jewish history and the Hebrew language, plus stacks of contemporary Israeli novels—and propped against them Sabbath candlesticks and Jewish ornaments, photographs of family at Jewish ceremonies, a Hanukkah menorah, alongside the dim, earnest light from the street—all of it seemed together and all at once to nod in agreement with Mrs. Bernstein, as if all the objects and texts might also break into applause.

—The wicked son is going to answer the door, said Scott.

He stood up, and in doing so knocked his fork and spoon onto the floor. He wanted to be the first to greet Moie Hamburger, who had arrived. We were all eager to see what cape, hat, or costume Moie was wearing. From where I was sitting I could see he was dressed in a maroon cowboy hat and vest, and recognized his strong laugh alongside Scott's. He was slender with a rugged face. Dark eyes, fat nose, patches of gray spread across thick hair and a pirate's goatee. Moie Hamburger held the Roto-Rooter franchise in Houston and was wealthy from unclogging drains and toilets. He was a bar-hopper, a party-crasher. Tonight, he was wearing tap shoes.

—Moie Mordecai Hamburger! You're late! You think you're Elijah! Moie! Get in here, Mr. Bernstein shouted and stood to bear hug his old friend.

My father and Dr. Rothman took the opportunity to knock back their tall glasses of red wine, and as they did my father's denim yarmulke fell off.

—*L'chayim*, Dr. Rothman said, raising his glass in a toast, and took another gulp.

Marcy laughed and gave Matt a look, after which both reached out to their silver cups of wine and dragged them closer to the edge of the table to sneak a sip when the next opportunity came. Mrs. Rothman stood to correct the settings atop a sideboard, dividing the little plates and large plates, the forks and knives.

Moie worked his way around the room, doffing his maroon Stetson, blowing air kisses, hugging the ladies especially tight, and then gathered himself to stand beside Dr. Rothman at the head of the table.

—I have made it. I bring the lights of *Pesach* to help guide us next year in Jerusalem! he said, and he reached under his vest and flicked a switch that started a set of blinking white lights fastened to the outside of his vest, dozens of them, about the size of peas.

As the lights blinked on and off, a great cheer went up. *L'chaim*, offered Mr. Bernstein, and the adults swigged more mouthfuls of wine. Matt and Marcy saw their chance and gulped down their glasses the way you might drink iced tea on a hot day. It was a charming dance, an awfully good pleasure that wandered easily around the room, as Moie patted shoulders and the tops of heads and took his seat.

Mother tapped her water glass with her spoon and began reminding Andrea that it was her turn to read. We moved through the story of Israel in the land of Egypt and counted out the ten plagues, dipping a finger into our wine and splashing drops onto our plates for each affliction. We raised our wine for the personal deliverance from slavery, our deliverance from sorrow to happiness, from mourning to rejoicing, from darkness to light, all in gratitude for the blessings and praise to God.

My brothers sat on opposite sides of Moie and both sat up straight, intent to be the muscle, and keep him in line. Moie had already drained and refilled his glass of wine. Scott looked at me, nodded in Moie's direction, and this time made the toking motion at the level of the table. Matt smiled. Oh, my, Marcy said, taking note, and she glanced in Moie's direction. When her grandmother looked at her, Marcy shrugged and took a sip of water. Grandma Selma raised her eyebrows quickly with a look that said, you kids think you are hardly noticeable.

Moie was already telling a story about how he'd gone

ice skating the day before in the Galleria Mall dressed as a priest, and he was waving aside efforts to resume the Seder. But his outfit was now in disarray. Lights began burning out and he was forced to turn off the switch that started up the blinking, which didn't upset his mirth one bit.

The Seder continued. We made a familiar melody as we went around the room. The give and takes of discussion were like defined trills. Dr. Rothman asking questions about our portion made him into a deep octave in the bass. All the other voices lofted over their recitation of the English portions and rolled across the chanting of the Hebrew portions with vigorous attention.

— You and Joe should come to Lincoln for a weekend. We'd have a splendid time, said Mr. Bernstein to my grandmother, before he took a shot from his wine glass and motioned to Mrs. Rothman for a refill.

— That would be splendid. It's been so long since we were there, she answered.

— You will come, won't you? We must arrange it before you leave tonight, Mrs. Bernstein said, and the two women touched each others's arms.

— Go where? asked my grandfather.

— Lincoln, darling.

— Well, yes.

Andrea stood and sang the lead for *Dayenu* in Hebrew. Her voice carried cool and pleasant. She sang rapidly, strong and clear, and without embellishment, about the kindnesses which the Lord extended to our ancestors, his pity and compassion, his dividing the Red Sea, his sending manna from heaven, giving us the Torah. Applause escorted her to her seat, and Moie—who had seemed on the edge of tears as Andrea sang and had leaned in closer to her and also had sang the *Dayenu* chorus the loudest, even flipping his blinking lights back on again and animatedly waved his arms like a concert conductor and holding his butter knife high—was still applauding when everyone else had stopped. When he could clap no more, he stood and motioned

Andrea to come over to him, seizing both her hands and pulling her tight for a hug, and saying Mazel tov! But he began to cough, spitting wads of phlegm into a napkin, and couldn't stop. Still he kept choking out, Mazel tov! Mazel tov!

—You have a lovely voice. I have never heard it sung so beautifully. Your voice is so bright, so shiny, my grandmother said to Andrea when she pulled away from Moie and sat down, and they smiled at each other.

—It's a wonderful voice, Mrs. Bernstein said, and seemed like she was about to cry.

Moie was standing now and putting on his coat. He couldn't stay, he said.

—Come now, after all that beautiful singing? Mr. Bernstein was trying to cajole him, and he patted his granddaughter Andrea on the head as he walked toward the foyer where Moie was saying goodbyes.

—I really must leave.

—I hope you enjoyed yourself, Mrs. Rothman said before hustling over to the kitchen to turn up the stove to rewarm something for the meal.

—Yes, entirely, always. Have a wonderful Seder, dears! This year in Texas! Next year, Jerusalem!

One by one we passed out the boiled and sliced eggs floating like buoys in the grainy salt water, and this was followed by bowls of matzah ball soup, which was followed by a tray of braised brisket, neatly trimmed in slices, seasoned with salt and plum sauce on a bed of butter leaf. Next came a serving bowl of *haroseth* with vinegar and apples and dried figs and pitted dates making a sweet aroma. I took an extra helping and did the same with the gefilte fish, each oblong whitefish spiced with onions and carrots lined on a silver tray atop more butter leaf. Then the side dishes. Spinach salad with mushrooms. Horseradish and beets. A dish of sweet potato and apple kugel.

Another salad of iceberg lettuce drowned in oil and vinegar. Pink butter-stewed radishes. A spring vegetable stew. Atop the sideboard were desserts, and at the center of them was a round tray of almond-walnut macaroons and a coconut macaroon cake.

At ease we ate and talked and praised the feeding. Noise, laughter, pass this, pass that, orders for more water, more kugel, more brisket, wine, and salt and pepper, and stray scoldings. Then came the second helpings, spoonfuls of vegetables and stew and the beets, the plates passed up and down the table, balanced from hand to hand. For each maker of each dish the praise was offered and seconded. These were followed by the appropriate demurrals. Mrs. Rothman was up and down without stop, hopping around the table. We quieted for a few moments and ate, until Marcy stood and ordered her mother to sit down, pointing an arm and forefinger at the assigned seat. Sit down, sit down, came a chorus of orders.

The grandparents talked of the proposed Tulsa-to-Lincoln weekend visit, how clean the air was in Nebraska, and what additions had been made to the synagogue there. The subject of conversation turned to Mr. Bernstein telling a story about a visitor to Shabbat services in Lincoln recently who had lived through the Warsaw Uprising.

—There wasn't enough bread, this fellow says, and so about one in the afternoon he walks out to one of the main streets to find some for his family. There were a lot of people and commotion. That's when he heard that three Germans had been killed. Started rounding people up, of course. Tanks coming into the streets, big as warehouses, this fellow says. Seemed like a peaceful day when you weren't near the commotion, he says. Can you believe that? People running in and out of courtyards to grab carts and wagons to make a barricade. And then he says, What I most remember is the aroma of dumplings and the rat-a-ta-ta-tat of machine guns.

I had not heard of the Warsaw Uprising, and listened closely to the portion about building barricades.

—This fellow says, he was in his apartment when someone put out a Polish flag, and the Germans starting firing at it. At the flag! Can you believe that? Just then there was a huge blast. The German tank had blown itself up. Apartment buildings that had been standing just a few seconds earlier were now gone, pile of rubble. The street was shrouded in a cloud of red dust. Trees and grass and bricks on the buildings were all covered in red dust. He says, women and children were running in every direction, covered in dust and powder. They kept coming and coming out of the bombed out areas, fleeing.

—What does the man do? my grandfather asked, after he'd been nodding with each new detail.

—He's an underwriter. How's that! He saw homes destroyed as a boy, and now he helps people obtain homes.

Someone asked my grandfather about High Holidays in Elma, the tiny Iowa town he moved to with his family, in 1920, when he emigrated from Ukraine.

—There used to be a synagogue in New Hampton, about 25 miles from Elma. Everybody who lived near that town used to come in, and they'd stay with people. You didn't go to a hotel. People would give up a bedroom or whatever there was. They slept on the sofa for a day or two. They went to shul both days. You didn't miss anything. See, you take in Elma, who was there? The Jews, I mean. The Dines. That's it. And us. Take Decorah, Iowa. There was just the Meyer brothers. They'd come into New Hampton. In Charles City, Oscar Barzuque would come in. In New Hampton already you had just enough to make a minyan. You know, twelve, fifteen men in that little synagogue. Of course at one time there were a lot of Jews in New Hampton, enough they were able to build a synagogue. Able to have a burial grounds. No rabbi, of course. But they had an old man there—I can't think, what's his name?—and he did all the davening or whatever you had on the holidays. We didn't need a rabbi. What was a rabbi? What did you need a rabbi for? You just davened. That's what you did. You prayed. All day. You'd start in the morning at eight o'clock and you wouldn't get through until about two o'clock in the afternoon. There weren't any speeches. Then you'd go back a couple hours later. You'd come back for *Mincha*. Dead tired, but you didn't rest.

—What did you think of Elma? Scott asked.

—Well you didn't think anything, son. You were glad to be here. Period. Anything else didn't matter. Nothing else mattered. There wasn't anything strange to me. I mean, it really didn't matter to me at all. We were glad to be in the United States. Period. Was glad to be in America.

A creamy yellow light fills the length of the windows, facing west, at the end of these shortening October days, as I write all this down in Portland.

All year Wendy and I tend a manageable garden, mostly with edibles planted to the umpteenth inch of our small lot. Apples, artichokes, blueberries, figs, grapes, raspberries, strawberries. Each June, in goes a planting of cucumbers, greens, hot peppers, and tomatoes.

This late in the afternoon the light whitens the ochre leaves of the butterfly bush and softens the wood of the back porch where our old white dog sleeps in a sunny spot. The light sifts between the last of the pink roses near the wilting tomato plants and through the skins of the fallen figs that our one-year-old black puppy hasn't chewed yet.

It's not quite brightness but a spongy flare over the neighborhood's rooftops that extends through the windows over the jam jar on the kitchen table where four exhausted sunflower cuttings sag like forgotten puppets.

By the time I settled in Portland, in 1995, I had lived in eight states in nine years.

It's clear to me that after all those separate moves—to a boisterous apartment in Boston where I turned twenty years old, an old farmhouse in Vermont, where I turned twenty-five, rickety digs in Washington, DC, where I turned thirty, a narrow San Francisco flat where I turned thirty-five, craftsman house in Portland where I turned forty, all those weeks and months putting a new household in order, arranging the dishes and clothing and books and furniture and artwork, marriage, fatherhood, divorce, and marriage again, teaching in one university followed by another, all the while orienting the days around becoming a writer—that the objects inside a house, moveable as they are, are the telling expressions of what we think of as home, more than the structures of the houses themselves.

Perhaps we're all building our concepts of home in stages, following the demands of the moment, and we may not live long enough to see how the sections fit together into a meaningful form.

If a home is a unique place, ostensibly only possible to experience when you are inside it, what does it mean that your memory of home, like a reproduction inside your mind, can be felt, or imagined, in any place, or every place, you go, inside the new homes you make, for any purpose?

And yet, why is it easy enough to write about that Seder night, in 1974, while also remaining comfortable within my resistance to its meanings and reasoned definitions, the fantastical telling of the old story of freedom and oppression where everyone comes through like representatives of a complete life of religious and observant Jews?

When I write all this out, in the dining room, in Portland, I find it helps to look down the long walnut table and be alert to the straight-back chairs surrounding it, the two sets of arm chairs in the room, mismatched side tables, mismatched lamps, portraits on the walls. It's at moments like this when I wonder, can a home only be in one place at one time?

As we remember our old homes, as we dream about them, imagine them, write about them—as I have done while working at a table Wendy and I bought together on NE Broadway Street in Portland, and the table is surrounded by chairs I bought with my first wife on Moraga Street in San Francisco, and the two arm chairs next to the dining room table are from my grandparents house on East 38th Street in Tulsa, and the table lamps are from the house on Loch Lomond in Houston, and two other arm chairs Wendy bought at a consignment shop in Portland after she came back to Oregon from law school in Washington, DC, long before we met—I'm seeing the contents of my history, our history, and various homes of that history, various lives and occasions, inside the context of my life.

As much as I enjoy their presence, thinking about these objects makes me feel I belong to no place, since I have removed them from the places that mark their meaning. Do all my homes reside in me? Perhaps no pilgrimage elsewhere is ever required.

And yet I'm creating a distorted facsimile of all these homes, just by writing about them. Aren't I?

What does that do to my understanding of the meaning of home as Texas?

And, what are the meanings these objects have acquired? Here, in this home, in Oregon? When these objects are placed in the dining room next to the wall? Or under the windows? How different are the meanings of the chairs around the dining room table, for instance, from their original location in the kitchen of the first-floor flat in the Sunset District in San Francisco where I first put them? Has the furniture multiplied its meanings? If so, it has also destroyed its original meaning in its original home.

Hasn't it?

Of course the furniture is silent.

My sitting at this Oregon table, in one of the California chairs, or looking at the Oklahoma armchairs, or the Texas lamps, is like a passage that connects me to every home I've known. Which makes me wonder whether, regardless of what I think of as unfolding time, if I'm living in all the homes at once?

Is that what it means to remember?

Because what I remember is, after Marcy opened the front door of the house on Rice Avenue, and we gazed in the direction of the threshold, and in Hebrew we invoked the prophet Elijah to aid God to direct his wrath upon evil and persecution and sought protection for the people of Israel against those who would destroy us, and we invited Elijah into our hearts to inspire us to love God and to build a good world of justice and freedom for all, and after I could feel the springtime humidity seep through the doorway and imagined above Houston a sky of drained silence as far as the eye could see, where the wrath of the Lord was about to fall, like a heavy hand, as it had in Egypt, and we spoke of the prophet Elijah's greatest mission to come, when the Messiah will appear on earth, to usher in the long-promised era of permanent tranquility and, with it, the arrival of peace for all men and women—after all that, and after all the singing of *Chad Gadya* and *Echad Mi Yodea* in both Hebrew and English, each to his own, some in tune, some at a whisper, some loud and out of tune, we all said good night and returned home at last to the house on Loch Lomond.

Once there I lay down on top of the bedcovers in my room and gazed up at the shadows on the ceiling. The wind was picking up outside. On the walls of the room light from the lamp above the garage flitted like a hummingbird. I heard my parents' voices in the kitchen in sharp volleys. Each voice held a mysterious gloom, a distant, felt darkness in the hoarse repetitions, the rough cadences.

Mother appeared at my doorway to say goodnight. She had a look on her face like she was walking on a path with small stones and had stopped to smell the intoxicating scent of a cluster of red flowers, breathing in deeply until she felt light-headed. My father appeared soon afterward, cracked the door and dropped a piece of black licorice into my hand.

The house was dark now. I left the desk lamp on. Outside the streetlights were dull, murky, and the heavy sky was fast in motion. Low clouds skimming the rooftops. I felt a bright pleasantness and could feel my thoughts bounding foolishly, as I hummed to myself one of the Haggadah's songs so that the memory of the Seder fell through me like a star. My pillow was askew under my head, and I was rubbing the corner of it with a hand, flicking the pillow case as the light from outside shimmered against the open curtains and flashed on the walls. I wondered when my brothers would return from wherever they were with friends, rattling through the crowded city as the hours carried forward, proud and happy to be on their own after leaving the Rothman's house early.

It was then I remembered Dr. Rothman standing in silence in his study before we left. He was setting books to one side of his desk with soft thuds and stacking the Haggadahs. He asked if I had a good time, and I nodded and could feel my heart thumping. A shaft of light from the street lit up the strewn papers on his desk. He looked at the light, too, I thought, but then turned his back to it. The books sat on the shelves like bricks in a wall—talmuds, commentaries, Hasidic histories, Yiddish tales—each book a link from the old shtetls of Europe and beyond, all the way to Texas, where households like his and ours gave direct thought to the writings, each word turned and leaned on.

I like to think I understood then that men like my grandfather and Mr. Bernstein and Dr. Rothman represented a life meant to catalogue Jewish thought, to gather into your house the Talmudic disputes and reckonings like manuscripts on a shelf, to know how to close your eyes and remember exactly which book held which sentence that recalled the moment which rabbi clarified what was a hat and what a cloak of understanding in Torah. It was as if these men could stare into the mirror and see not their own eyes but dates of history and the etymologies of Hebrew back to the ancient days. Time shimmered in that mirror, passions shimmered, accounts of thousands of years of Jewish characterizations of truth and how to live by it shimmered. The faces of the ghostly past and the living worlds were unaltered there, tethered to this night.

Soon I leaned forward in bed feeling tired but not weak and stared out the window at the rose bushes planted in the patio next to the garage. An annoyance crept into me at my ardor. I feared mastering one form of knowledge at the expense of others, and didn't know exactly what that meant. It was a brutal thought. Quickly I wished I was a more generous person, and tried to put the misery out of my head, though perhaps I was astonished that I could find these puzzling thoughts arousing. The thoughts glimmered inside me, then broke loose and hid themselves inside a dull anger.

Had I known this was a moment of shame? Did I know how delicate, humiliating, it was, this thought of turning away from the Jewish world in search of secret knowledge that didn't come from the dead but from the living works of life, from the joy and desire of new life—even if all that was vulgar, full of lust and pity? I simply tried, at that age, to feel indifferent, though later I would feel vindictive toward all that knowledge on the bookshelf, and would see it as a stooped world.

At once I stood and paced the floor, then sat down on the bed with my bare feet flat on the carpet.

Velvet came into the room and lay down with a thump. I sat beside her and patted behind her ears. When I heard footsteps outside the house and the sharp banging of bottles tossed into the metal garbage can, I flung myself onto the bed. It was one of my brothers come home. He unlocked the back door next to my room, opened and closed it lightly, and poked his head in. It was Matt.

—Why're you still up?

—No reason.

—They gone to bed? he asked, and we looked at each other as I nodded.

He shut the door and walked down the hallway through the kitchen. I lay back down on the bed and breathed through my open mouth. I felt a strange pain enter me, like a sore, and decided to brave it till it dissolved. My eyes moved across the room. I was still dressed, with my tie on, lying on top of the covers, my forehead moist. The Seder was falling away. The minutes ticked dismally on. The madness of the future, like a checkered shadow on the walls and ceiling, was locked in my heart. Sleep was gathering in my eyes. All the wayward forms of the night flickered.

Soon Scott opened and closed the back door and slipped quietly into the house. A hot wind tapped against the window. The dull light from above the garage was out now. And so the dark air appeared through an opening in the curtain to be silver. The night's heat weighed heavily over the empty streets and the thick spears of grass and every part of Meyerland where families all night long had remembered their bondage in Egypt. The heat drifted over the slender sidewalks and flower beds. The heat swooned over the calm waters of the bayou. And for hours until morning the springtime heat, like the angel of death skimming over the slanted rooftops farther into time, passed over us.

The Quarrel

Our trouble began when the rabbi led me through the small hallway and the door of his office.

This was April, 1976, a month after my father's stroke, the year I was twelve. I'd been sent by the school principal after playing hooky in the synagogue's empty kitchen, wandering behind silver refrigerators and stoves alongside the many cabinets for meat and dairy dishes, racks of table cloths, and folding chairs by the hundreds. Afterward, I'd snuck into the deserted sanctuary. I sat in the front row, where it didn't take long for my ears to adjust to the quietness. Nothing of the blazing hot weather outside was noticeable. I looked through the dim light at the ark. The long curtain was open. Torahs exposed. Stained-glass motif of the burning bush exposed. The tranquility was not difficult to catch hold of, and I was fully absorbed by it.

—Will you take a seat, please. Make yourself comfortable. I'll be right back, the rabbi said, once I arrived in his office.

I took notice of the colored spines on the books on his shelves, even though the room was poorly lit. Over his desk hung a painting of the Western Wall in Jerusalem, a picture which, he once told me, he loved because it is the place of all learning, all suffering, and all perfection. I looked at the wall in the painting and the image of the rabbi and other men davening. Even then I knew I was supposed to be aware of the tragic beauty in their prayer, that the act of prayer was the height of enjoyment of life.

I liked when the rabbi talked to me privately. Better than his classroom teaching, a traditional form of questions and answers. Better than his sermons, though they held my attention. His sermon about realizing inner strength by reaching out toward God might include a quote from Psalms: "My help is from the Lord, the maker of heaven and earth." Once he spoke of a Baptist gentleman from West Texas who wanted to attend a Shabbat service. The rabbi told him, any time you want to attend my service, I'll meet you at the door and welcome you in, for my house, as it says in Isaiah, will be called a house of prayer for all people.

And yet it did not seem as if the rabbi was wrestling with some internal combustion of ideas or beliefs himself. Not once did I view him as a genius from a special world or imagined his daily existence as remote from the concerns of an orderly family life. What was he like at home? I don't think I ever asked the question. Did he speak often or seldom to his wife? Were they anxious or calm together? Did they have secrets from each other? How many? Was his study where he wrote his sermons private? Was she permitted to enter? Or their children? Was his wife included or excluded from his interior life? Was their conversation one of banter or bickering? I kept a veil over all that, not so much baffled by the rabbi's life as much as I must have not been intrigued by it, painfully uncurious about his joys and sufferings. I knew nothing of his friendships, if any, and assumed that the congregation provided him company and comfort. But he did carry within him a need to communicate a rush of ideas, often stated as platitudes or quotations from Torah, and he rode atop that talk like he was leading a tribe across a desert that seems to have no idea of a world beyond the next hill, beyond the flocks and herds and imperatives of nomadic life.

T hat's what it felt like, three years earlier, during the afternoon *Musaf* service on Yom Kippur, in 1973, when I was nine, when the rabbi and I ran into each other in the crowded hallway.

Mother had said I could take a forty-five minute break from the day-long prayer service, and a dozen of us boys from the

Day School gathered outside the shul with a football. After we all agreed on what would be the last play, Michael Friedman took the snap and drifted back under the warm sun, his necktie loosened and blowing above his shoulder. We needed a miracle. The score stood 12-7. Our side was down, and Friedman was going for broke. To get free of four other boys, all of us dressed in slacks and button-down shirts and ties, I aimed for the sidelines, then cut a diagonal upfield. I was running hard, but thinking we didn't have any chance to win the game. Glancing behind me, I could see Friedman's curly hair as he pump-faked, then let the ball loose. Over the grass the ball lofted. Someone was grabbing my shirt among a crowd of boys near the end zone—pushing, and leaning, and pulling, while the ball wobbled toward all of us. But it appeared to be coming in short. I cut in and made the catch, trapping the ball against my hip. Two boys overran the play and fell down around me.

I backed into the end zone for six.

On our triumphant return inside the shul, after we started calling the play, the Yom Kippur Hail Mary—they're going to be talking about it for as long they're talking about Yom Kippur, one of them said—Friedman and I ran into Rabbi Segal in the corridor near the atrium. He offered us a pleasant look, waved us over, and I could smell his breath from a mint he was chewing, and his aftershave. He favored precocious students, is what he often said, and when I got into trouble at school and sent to his office for reprimand, he would send me back to class with an aphorism, something like, Remember, the truth stands up, but a lie does not.

—Anyone I know out there playing football with you boys? asked the rabbi, meaning his oldest son.

—No, sir, Friedman said, with mock furtiveness, because the rabbi's son had been in the scrum defending the end zone on the last play.

Thousands of people were walking in the narrow halls. There were men in dark suits and ladies in new dresses and jewelry—as if what was required for inscription in the Book of

Life was being the best-dressed Chosen People of Texas. To accommodate everyone, some five-thousand families, there was an early and late service. The Orthodox chapel held a service for two hundred people, and the school auditorium seated another seven hundred people, mostly young families, where the synagogue installed a projection screen to show the main sanctuary's service. Mounted speakers broadcast the prayers into the hallways.

All that day, inside the shul there'd been a hum as congregants listened through small earpieces to transistor radios, stuffing themselves with reports of the war against Israel, started that day on two fronts, by Syrians in the Golan Heights, and by Egyptians in the Sinai. We'd heard reports that, even as sirens overtook all other sounds in Jerusalem and Haifa and Tel Aviv and across Israeli villages, Yom Kippur davening continued in thousands of bomb shelters. Army trucks drove through the streets picking up soldiers. I would read later in the *Jewish Herald Voice,* delivered to our house every Thursday, that in one Jerusalem neighborhood the driver asked for a man to come out of the makeshift shul. With his wife beside him, he took off his tallit, and his kittel, and placed them in his wife's hand, stepped onto the truck, and left with other soldiers. By nightfall Israel would be in a total blackout. The shutters of apartments and houses pulled down. The power to traffic lights and street lamps cut off.

Friedman and I were talking to the rabbi through the din. You fellows do *tashlich* this year? he asked. We told him how ten days before, around Rosh Hashanah, Friedman and I scurried into the switchgrass down the slope of the bayou among the armadillos and garter snakes and emptied our pockets of lint and tossed them into the trickle of brown water, mouthing the prayer of repentance. That's the spirit, the rabbi said. Be strong and courageous, boys.

After I'd returned to my family in the crowded sanctuary, when the president of the synagogue took to the microphone, he said something from the bimah none of us had heard before.

Speaking about the fighting that day in Israel, he pledged a million dollars to support the Israeli defense effort. He implored everyone to go home and write a check—this very day, he said, before you break your fast, before you put your children safely to bed—even though handling money was forbidden on Yom Kippur. Cash dollars are needed in this, our most desperate hour, he called out and pounded the lectern. Give until it hurts. Give as if Golda Meier has asked you herself on this, our Day of Atonement.

All around us men squinted, as if concentrating on a difficult thought. Women leaned over children. Hands whisked through the air, and, as if passing through a gauntlet, hundreds stood and walked to the exits.

Three nights later, Mayor Louie Welch opened a speech from the Beth Yeshurun bimah to nearly four thousand people who'd come to an emergency rally for all the Jewish congregations in the city to hear the Israeli Consul report on the progress of the war, while outside, on Beechnut Street, in front of a row of brick apartments, stood a band of anti-Israel picketers, holding signs that said—

THE PLIGHT OF THE PALESTINIANS =
THE PLIGHT OF THE MEXICANS IN TEXAS
HITLER WAS RIGHT!!

The shul's Men's Club had rounded up a handful of Israeli graduate students who were living in the city and studying at the University of Houston to come to the synagogue and be security for the rally. Those who joined the protection unit were rumored to be members of the Houston branch of the JDL. When an older gentleman, a Holocaust survivor, came hollering out of the apartments on Beechnut Street while waving a baseball bat, the counter-demonstrators moved onto Beth Yeshurun's property. That's when a wiry Israeli student charged them, his blue knitted yarmulke pinned to his black hair. A beefy protestor clocked the Israeli in the ear, and the

Israeli staggered back. There was a swift boot to the Israeli's chest. Quickly he recovered and punched the protestor in the eye, followed by squeezing his throat until the man began to gag.

Out from under people's shirts came axe handles and broom sticks and steel pipes, followed by bloody heads and shirts. When the scuffle was over, the air felt like ash over everyone's hair and faces. The counter-protestors had fled. The police arrived late. People were standing outside the synagogue, ordinary people, bent over with convulsive sobbing.

—How many times are we going to do this? You skipping class like this. You're in sixth grade. You should know better, the rabbi said, after he returned to the office, stood over me, blocking my way, his hands shoved into the pockets of his trousers, speaking quickly, removing his coat to sit behind his desk, then looking away as if looking directly at me blunted his mood.

I didn't answer, tried to smile, and shrugged.

—You're bored? Is that it? That's what I'm told. Are we not interesting enough for you? The best rabbi is the heart, son. The best teacher is time. The best book, next to Torah, is the world. The best friend is God. If you can learn that, and agree to accept rules, such as stay in your class, stay in the school wing, don't go into the janitors' quarters, don't hide in the kitchen or in the sanctuary—you know that's off limits during school hours—God's will, you will reach your potential. I saw your father in the hospital just yesterday. Did you know that? He is doing much better. Much better. Said the *Sh'ma* with him. I said it for us both. Do you think that'll help him? What do you understand about the *Sh'ma*? I want to know. Tell me. Please.

—It's rolled inside every mezuzah, I said, referring to the small parchment fixed to the doorpost of Jewish homes as a sign and reminder of their faith.

He wriggled his fingers with both hands for me to say more.

—It's about, you know, oneness of God, and the kingdom of God, and the importance of performing deeds. I guess, Jewish deeds. OK. To say *Sh'ma* every day, when you wake up, when you go to bed. It's inside the tefillin. Right? And, it's a reminder of the story, I guess, of the Exodus.

He was watchful, then noticed something out the window that surprised him, and held his attention.

—And the freedom to love God. Don't forget. The freedom to love God. I said to your father, Live well, it's the greatest revenge.

That made me laugh, because my father, who had been in the hospital for several weeks then, was still experiencing great difficulty hearing and speaking, and mostly sat crumpled in his bed in his green hospital gown. He was forty-six years old and unable to point to pictures of common objects like shoes and cups, even when they were named by the nurse, or to discriminate between paired pictures, like dogs and cats, forks and spoons. Silent in his bed but for grunts and stray words, he was able to point correctly to only a few letters of the alphabet.

A few days before I got in trouble in the sanctuary and sent to speak with the rabbi, I'd been at the hospital after school, standing in a corridor near the waiting room, listening to an older white woman, with a gray ponytail threaded through the back of a ball cap, talk about her slippers. She was sipping Coca-Cola in a glass bottle through a straw. Mother was meeting with doctors, and I was told to wait outside the intensive care ward. Tugging on her hospital gown and cinching the belt tighter, the women kicked her slippers on and off as she talked. They were terry cloth blue and one of them hand a hole in the toe. I was seized by a high fever, she was saying, and I couldn't breathe for days—and she was making a choking motion with both hands against her neck. A television set in a patient's room nearby was playing a rerun of *The Rifleman*. Hospital workers walked past in groups, and the fluorescent light sprawled across the chairs and work stations. These gosh darn slippers, she said, pulling them off and laying them in her lap like a slender purse.

Just then Rabbi Segal stepped out of one of the patient rooms. He appeared troubled. But when he saw me, he walked over to say hello.

—See your father today? he asked.

—I'm not allowed in there.

—To be kind is better than to be right, he said and seemed to wonder what I was doing talking to the old woman.

—Ma'am, this is my rabbi.

—I'm Baptist, child. Not sure I qualify for y'all. I do believe God created the entire world. You believe that, rabbi? Don't you?

—Yes, sweetie, said the rabbi, and she nodded back, her face aggrieved, while he walked over to speak to a hospital worker he seemed already to know, and didn't return.

—Your daddy in here, child, is that it? He's going to keep living, I know it. Between your God and my God, he's going to be fine. I'll be praying, child.

She reached out to squeeze my hand, and I let her take it.

—We Texans stick together.

—Yes, ma'am.

—Love them Longhorns.

With my forefinger and pinky I raised the Hook 'em Horns sign.

—Now you're talking. Let's go, Horns! My daddy was a football player in high school. Cancer killed him. Died in my mother's arms. Boy, he tried and tried to live. Cancer got him. I remember he was laying there the last days. Wouldn't drink no water. Fool. But it wouldn't have saved him. That ever happen to you, you force that water down your daddy's throat. Promise me now, she said, and she coughed hard, and then sat with her mouth open until her nurse arrived.

Mother reappeared down the hallway, tapping her watch.

—I was looking everywhere for you, I was worried sick. Who

was that woman? she asked when we stepped into the elevator.

—She said she needed a nurse. I was trying to help her.

—Don't be so trusting of people you don't know. She could have been contagious. I don't have time for you to get sick. I don't have time to worry about you, she said and we whirled through the automatic doors toward the crowded parking lot.

Now, in the rabbi's office, he suddenly stood, and shuddered, like a willow tree bending over a current, rocking in place.

—You're not an easy one. You know that? You have something, the rabbi said, sitting back down behind the desk.

—What do you mean? When you say, something?

—Do you know what your teachers are saying about you? Take a guess. It doesn't require much imagination. If we'd all known what we know now, that you'd be bored and wander off, perhaps it would've been better for you to go to public school all this time. We don't want you to leave. Of course not. But what's with this playing hooky? he said, walking near to where I was sitting, and leaning on his desk.

—What do they say?

—They say what I've been telling you. Telling you many years since you were just a *pisher*. You've got a knack. As the Torah says, You understand a man by his deeds and words. I'm warning you. I would hate to see you turn your back. That would be big trouble. Big trouble. Not like this. Big trouble. You know, when I was starting out being a rabbi, I wanted to know as much as possible. See? Aren't you like that? Don't you want to be like that? Tell me, what do you think about when you're praying?

—I just chant it the way I feel it.

—Favorite story in Torah these days? he asked, and returned to his chair and sat down, leaned forward, cleared several pencils away and rolled them into a top drawer.

—King David.

—Oy, King David. Don't put yourself in the way of temptation, young man. Even the father of Solomon could not resist it.

—I like all that.

—That's not an answer.

—What do you want to know?

—You like when people have trouble?

The question startled me, but I said nothing.

—Bored in school? Are you? That's what I'm told. That's what you said. Bored in school. What kinds of thoughts do you have? When you're bored? he said and eyed me like he was waiting for something dramatic to happen.

I was feeling that aura I'd felt at my grandmother's funeral. That I could dream two worlds at once. Everything not in the room except the two of us appeared to fade away. It's here, too, in the retelling, now that I am more acquainted with a face like the one the rabbi was showing, that I can see seeds of the debacle that would take place between us. The rabbi seemed to believe he was the rabbi of ordinary children who grew up in safety, in comfort, and who knew sorrow only in superficial forms. He believed we held too close to trivial concerns. But here I was, and it was different. Perhaps he was looking to challenge me back to an attentiveness he knew he had helped to cultivate. He was staring, and I stared back, focusing on the folds in his cheeks, on his trim, gray sideburns. If someone had knocked at the door, neither of us would have heard. We had positioned ourselves as if on a high bridge.

—Stuff like, why am I myself and not someone else? You know. I think about that. About, am I actually me? When did my thoughts start and when do they end?

—You've got your head in the clouds, son.

—Stuff like that. Just, you know.

—Come back down to earth. Go back to class.

I didn't waste any time to think but sprang up, and I hoped he was no longer disappointed in my life. He took hold of his coat and followed me down the hall. I could feel him walking slowly, trailing me. He was breathing heavily, but we were both walking measuredly. Then the rabbi sped up, put a palm on my shoulder and patted me, before at last he turned to walk out of the building. Once back in school, I lowered myself in a seat next to my friends and sat there still as a mountain.

Nineteen-eighty. Nineteen-eighty-one. The years blend together. Days of insolence, days of heat.

During a discussion of the *Akedah*, the story of Abraham's binding of Isaac, the rabbi set us up in our high school Hillel class so one side argued what kind of God would ask a man to murder his own son, while the other side contended one must fear God to have faith in God.

Around the open chapel were so many of my friends from the Day School, all of us attending the upper-level Jewish studies classes at the synagogue while also going to the neighborhood's public high school, a school so populated with Jewish students that classes were cancelled during High Holidays. For most people in the rabbi's high school classes, Judaism held the truths of life—and life, as they saw it, was given meaning by Jewish codes and interpretations. They didn't see Torah as a hindrance, but an opening to the mysteries of thought. If learning to interpret existence could have a root, Judaism was it. There wasn't much questioning of that. It didn't appear hidden or perplexing. The classes were offered like a gift of a Jewish dream with ancient scenes and theatricality.

Standing with his arms crossed, the rabbi encouraged one side, then the other to contradict. But, it became too much for him. Quoting from Maimonides, he immersed us in the exuberance of his argument that God accepts Abraham's willingness to offer his son as the highest expression of faith.

—Abraham must be revered, precisely for going through with the test to sacrifice his one and only son. That's another way to think of the famous answer—*Hineni*, behold, here I am—that Abraham makes to God when God first calls him to the binding, the *Akedah*. Here I am, Abraham says, present and accounted for, prepared to do your bidding, said the rabbi.

—It wasn't his only son, I said, raising my hand, while my friends rolled their eyes.

—True, the rabbi agreed but didn't elaborate.

—I read that the binding of Isaac was a way to end child sacrifice, Gail Gerber said with a tone of empathy.

—To end child sacrifice? That's correct. The purpose of telling the story is to help those in later times put an end to that practice. Abraham is partly responsible for that.

—But that's not why he's celebrated. He's praised, not for ending child sacrifice, but for his willingness to go through with the killing, she answered.

Wriggling his fingers, the rabbi indicated she say more.

—And that's what makes him the Father of Judaism? And Islam? And Christianity?

—Father of Christianity? That's like being the Father of Texas, Friedman said and we all laughed.

—Besides if people wanted to stop child sacrifices they could have just done it. They could have prohibited it. My question is, anyway, where is Sarah during all this? Gail said.

—Exactly. Why is Sarah shunted to the side while Abraham has a special relationship with God? I said.

—I don't think a mother would have agreed to it. Not my mother anyway, Gail said.

—The *Akedah* demonstrates Abraham as a model of moral faith, said the rabbi.

—That could justify anything. Murder, war, anything, I said.

—Rape, said Gail.

—The *Akedah* is done for God's sake, to please God, said the rabbi.

—Is God playing a joke? Why would God find that pleasing? Is faith to God required to be a Jew? asked Patti Epstein in a flat drawl.

—Go on, sweetie, said the rabbi.

—Imagine, a man down the street kills his son and in trial claims that God told him to. We'd think he was insane. Even if he had all the right religious arguments. We'd still convict him of murder.

— But we might let him off if we thought he was insane so that he could serve his sentence outside of prison, the rabbi said, and he seemed to understand where Patti's thinking led and moved to debate her.

— Was Abraham insane? Patti asked.

— We must accept that God did speak to him, said the rabbi.

— How did he know it was God? How would Abraham have been sure it was God speaking and not his conscience? Patti answered.

— Maybe he's a fanatic. Abraham hears voices, but it might not be God's. The voices tell him, command him, to do something that violates decency, I said.

— Moral law, Patti added.

— Moral law. OK? It's incompatible with morality. Then no matter how amazing the voices are, how God-like, no matter how convincing, Abraham had to consider it fake, an illusion. You know. But he goes through with it anyway, I said.

— That's crazy, said Patti.

— Not only that. Anyone could read into this portion by saying, look, there's this huge magnificence in the world and there appears to be an ordering force to it all. That's what we're reading in Donin's *How To Be a Jew*. Right? But you're saying that this force, God, Yahweh, can actually intervene. That God actually cares about what it is we do here, what we eat and don't eat, insists on all this praise every single day.

— Praise, praise, praise, Friedman sang out.

— What's with God's self-esteem anyway? And always caring about who wins and loses all these wars, and stuff like that, and the special interest in the Jews. How can we ever possibly know what the big force is in the universe? Is there only one? The mystery is interesting. Isn't it? Not knowing. Right? How can any human being possibly know? How can you not just want to discard it all? I said.

— There's a big hole in the bagel, Friedman coughed out to

laughter in the chapel, alluding to Rabbi Segal's pet aphorism to pay attention to important matters over trivial ones, to focus on the bagel, he liked to say, not the hole.

—Abraham is expected not just to believe in God, but it's like a cult, with a leader who demands love and fear every hour of the day, I said.

—That's enough, the rabbi said.

—It's *1984*, said Friedman.

—Exactly. God is Big Brother. Besides, it isn't God who made Judaism. We did, and we keep making it every day, I said.

—That's enough.

—We know people make religion because we know people who think they have God's permission to commit any atrocity in God's name. All these zealots and terrorists.

—Enough.

—The KKK, Patti Epstein said.

—The KKK don't give religion a peaceful reputation, Friedman said.

The rabbi closed his eyes, breathed in through his nostrils, sighed, then opened his eyes to look at us all.

—One's personal experiences shape the issues that you confront as Jews. They shape your perspective. The same holds for Abraham. The *Akedah* is the supreme example of self-sacrifice in obedience to God's will. We don't know if there was this actual situation in Abraham's life. I grant you that. But the story demonstrates the dilemma every Jewish person must go through and overcome to be a faithful Jew. We are imprinted to stay as one people, the Chosen People. What would you sacrifice to show God your faith?

The answers were shouted back. Television. A football game. A sister. And that was that. After class the rabbi left immediately without a word.

Side by side Gail and I walked out to the parking lot.

—If it was my mother instead of Sarah, God wouldn't have stood a chance, she said.

—Totally. I'd put money on my mother over God every

time, I said, and we laughed uncontrollably, then walked across Beechnut Street to a convenience store to meet up with friends.

For a time I was enlivened by debates like that, as if a new verbal energy was coming into my mouth.

I would wander from my house over to the bayou and its milky, brown waters and walk the footpath, the same route we took during the Exodus reenactments. Inside my head I was debating the rabbi. No longer just saying my part, but mocking his.

You think you've got it all figured out? God? he'd say. God is too funny, I'd say. Are you laughing at God? he'd say. I'm laughing at the whole shebang, I'd say. You're changing the subject, he'd say. I don't sleep with God under my pillow, I'd say. Oh, you've got an answer for everything, he'd say. Now you're changing the subject, I'd say, because you can't defend God. God doesn't need to be defended, he'd say. Then why all this defense? Why all the training and schooling and prayer and the Sisterhood and the Men's Club and this stuff about what God says, what God means, what it means to be Jewish, to live with Jews, to live with non-Jews, to be a good Jew this, to be a good Jew that? I'd say, and not just in my head but out loud, into the humid air. Because that's what we do here, he'd say. Indoctrinate, I'd say?

I floated in a reverie, a mixture of wooziness and ferocity—like when you're the only person in the street before dawn after being up all night—astonished, empowered, making up this new passionate voice inside my head, with so much delight, yet with an abiding uncertainty. With the bayou trickling alongside me under a scorching wind, with only instinct, determination, and craving for the pleasures of the words and their significances.

Following the debate about the *Akedah* in Torah class, I accompanied my girlfriend, Shelly Rose, to Saturday morning services at shul. It was near the anniversary of her mother's death, two years earlier.

Shelly was sixteen, a year younger than me—a shy girl, with dark hair, pretty and detached, with a contented authority to her gaze. We had been a thing almost from the first day we met, three years earlier, when I first saw her tangled among a group of girls on the edge of a dance floor at a bar mitzvah party. The tables of the hotel banquet room were decorated with photos of the bar mitzvah boy at different times of his life. A few days after his birth, his head large and bald. In football pads or Little League uniform. Year after year his face narrowing with each new team. There was a sparkling globe spinning above us, the DJ playing something like "Sir Duke." The brass trumpets and saxophones swinging to a funky drumbeat. Shelly and I simply stood there, staring. It hardly lasted anytime at all, as boys and girls rushed to the floor, shaking in time. Girls in tube tops and barefoot. Boys in hush puppies and open-collared shirts. All of the dancers squinting against the up tempos. Torsos twisting. Hips and hamstrings. Thighs and calves. Bare arms shifting up and down to the music.

All the dance long there was a sincere delicacy about Shelly, and also remoteness. But mostly a sense that a matching face was looking back at my own with a shuddering spirit. As the party wore on there grew a bashful madness between us.

A few weeks after the dance, for three days, we planned over the telephone to meet outside the Jewish Community Center so I could walk her home on the footpath along Brays Bayou. Up you go, she said with a high drawl when she found me where I was sitting on a bench near the front stairs. She wore blue jeans, a blouse buttoned almost to the neck and a thin silver necklace. We walked alongside the water past joggers and cyclists and elderly couples exercising. The horizon hung in the distance. I could feel the skin of her fingers rub against the skin of my hand.

We talked easily for the half hour it took to arrive near the corner of her street on the west side of Hillcroft, when she said, plain as could be, You look sad. Right now, you look sad, she said. Why do you say that? I said. I don't know. Are you? Do you feel sad? Nothing wrong with that, she said, and smiled.

We stood there, waiting for something to happen, while all along I was glad she noticed something about my spirit. It lifted me, as if she was saying our yearnings had every reason to exist. All around us the houses lay peacefully, the roofs slanting in a gentle silence under fading streaks of light. Without daring to touch each other's face or hair or to place a hand on the other's hip or behind the waist, we simply hovered there, like a wispy fragrance. We both sensed the secret, a presence leaping back and forth between us, as if time could be forgotten, impossible to measure, warm, and ghostly, like feeling someone's breath on your skin.

When finally we stopped in front of her house, Shelly peeked over her shoulder, and I thought I caught a glimpse of her mother in the dining room window where she moved back and forth, distinctly tremulous, opaque, like a reflection of a shadow floating between two worlds. The lawns shined in all their mowed, diagonal lines. Each blade of grass appeared to be staring in our direction.

Before services began, that Saturday morning, Shelly disappeared to talk to her girlfriends near the little Orthodox chapel. I wandered alone toward the offices along the corridor of the main sanctuary.

When I think about what happened next, I see the paradox. The myth of one's great crisis is precisely that which we come to trust the most. We absorb the myth into our identity and preserve it when it comes under threat, such that we have a devotion, a tenderness even, for the darker occasions of our testimony.

—Ready to pray? the rabbi called cheerfully, his voice startling me from a direction I hadn't noticed near an office desk, while he was looking into a reflective window and adjusting his tie, twisting his chin in a fashion that let me notice how long his graying sideburns were.

— Yep. Ready, I said and pumped a fist.

— How's school?

— Midterms, I said.

— Have you read this morning's *parashah*? he said, using the Hebrew word for the portion of the Torah assigned for the week's reading.

— No, sir. No.

— Just like you.

— Sir?

— You hesitate. Remarkable.

He was fiddling with his tie. In his eyes I could see he believed his unshakable duty was to prepare us to know — these were his words — the right way and wrong way and nothing in the gray as we ascended to Jewish adulthood. You hesitate. Remarkable. I heard the words, but to me they said, you are not invited to point out your inadequacies. You are not invited to form yourself to your own limits beyond the traditional habits and insecurities about what is good or not for the Jews. You are not invited to forge yourself.

— You don't know what to do right now. Do you? If you say what you want to, you're worried I'll react. Is that it? the rabbi said, suddenly undoing his tie and starting over.

— Is this a game?

— Are you playing one?

— What's it feel like, praying the way you do? I asked.

— Perhaps you'll find out.

I tucked my knitted tallit bag, with a Star of David stitched in blue, under my arm, like a folded newspaper. I felt diminished as if I was falling out of love.

— You read all the books in your office? I said.

— No, I just keep them to impress all my students. And to remind me that life is difficult.

— Really? Don't need a book for that.

—What's the first key to praying? he said after we'd been silent, and I had been watching him rework the knot in his tie.

—To pray.

—Not to think?

—That comes later.

—Thinking is where we understand the truth, he said and patted the front of his shirt.

—What about those who don't understand the words?

—You must help them. God can't be everywhere all the time. God needs God's people to take care of the other people.

—Like a rabbi?

—Yes.

—What if they're afraid of the words? What if they don't understand, and they just settle on their assumptions about everything?

—Perhaps they'll go far with that, and then farther.

—Further.

—What?

—Further. Not distance, degree.

—We'll need you to take an aliyah this morning. All right? An usher will find you. Shabbat Shalom, he called, and turned to walk into the sanctuary to open the morning's service.

On the bimah I nudged my way toward the lectern alongside three men bent over the Torah and awaited my turn to chant the aliyah before the Torah reading. My tallit snug around my shoulders and the fringes of the tzitzit lingering past my waist. Black yarmulke pressed to the back of my head. Flakes of dust covered the laminated card with the Hebrew prayer I was set to recite. But I knew the words from heart. When my turn came, I pressed the tzitzit to the crooked letters on the parchment scroll and kissed the fringes, adjusted the microphone, and bounced the words out of my mouth, at first calmly, and then flung them outward toward the congregants, hoping to make everyone shiver with the prayer that looks backward and forward at once, recalls a lost past of the Israelites in the desert as they move from one encampment to the next after fleeing

Egypt. My drawl deep and clear, so that when I reached the last words, *noten-ha-torah*, I held them lazily through the sanctuary's cooled air like a flock of swallows drifting over everyone's heads.

After I stepped off the bimah and buttoned my suit jacket, a few men in suits and ties stopped me to shake my hand.

Shelly patted my arm when I sat down beside her. Not sure what any of that means anymore, I whispered and crossed my arms. Well, we're here, she said, with a flat stare, appended to a frown, appearing determined, measured, with a searching look like she was waiting for weather to arrive and she could taste a quickening in the air.

Men and women scattered throughout the sanctuary stood to say the Mourner's Kaddish. Smoothing her skirt, Shelly stood, too, lifting her right heel onto her left toe, and held the prayer book with both hands underneath it. The Hebrew words dangled from her lips, her eyes twitching, her head looped low, as if a distant echo might knock her over.

That day, in springtime, the day of the quarrel with the rabbi—when I was seventeen, in the presence of my oldest friends, kids I'd known since nursery school—I was feeling distant and disenchanted, aroused by my own righteousness as I was biking to shul after days of rain and flooding. I was stewing over the rote-ness, if not the rottenness, of my weekly Torah studies. The rabbi had a stack of arguments, I thought, but did I really have to argue back with him? Have this ancestral argument with God? Or with God's representative? He could say whatever he wanted, but I didn't have to be there to hear it. Did I? I suppose the rabbi thought, of late, he saw an expression of meanness in my eyes, certainty not perplexity. I suppose the rabbi thought I was bewildered.

Is that right?

Did he think my eyes were expressing certainty? Because, in

my head, it was the opposite. I wasn't trying to say, I am. But, am I?

And yet, too, I was unlocking a secret, like sniffing at strong winds that had come from miles away. I wanted to be carried away on those winds past the horizon, part wanderer, part fugitive.

Perhaps if he would have conceded a point.

But, it was me who wouldn't concede a point, interrogating every word.

—Ladies and gentlemen, remember these words. *Ga-dol Ha-shem Um-hu-lal-me-yod; Veleg-du-lato, Ain-chaker.* Great is the Lord, praised above all, but his greatness is hidden. Let's begin with a simple question. What does it mean that God's greatness is hidden? asked the rabbi, calling on me.

—You can't search for it. I mean, you could try. But it's only found in deeds. Prayers. Keeping traditions. That kind of thing, I said, dutifully, with what I took to be nonchalance.

—And, community. Right? And, community.

The rabbi asked if I could relate another verse to the coming Passover. The verse was from *Ashrei*—"The Lord is good to all, and his tender mercies are over all his works"—and he said it in English without quoting the Hebrew. He waited for me to answer, alert, I felt, to any infestation of doubt.

—I don't think I can answer that one, rabbi, I said, although I knew I was expected to speak of God's vastness and appreciate his goodness as king and caring ruler who deserves praise from his people and all humanity, and to identify God's greatness in hearing the cries of the children of Israel in Egypt and delivering us from bondage, and to praise God's existence in the Ten Commandments and in the renewed covenant God makes with Moses.

—Take it easy. Why shouldn't you? You know the answer. Try this. How was God good to the children of Israel while they wandered for forty years in the desert?

This time he didn't wait and asked the class to write answers in our notebooks. When he arrived at my desk to see what I was scribbling, the rabbi pressed my body back from how I was covering the paper, stiffly passed his fingers over the words I'd written there, and rested both hands on my shoulders.

—I suppose you want to read that to us? he said before walking in front of the chapel and taking a position with his eyes on me.

—Not really.

—I think we'd all be interested. Do you have a problem? Do you lack something?

—No problem.

—Do you not understand where you are?

—Here I am.

—That's funny? Read it. Read it out loud. Don't be so sensitive. Faith provides roots for those who doubt. Have you ever planted a garden at home?

—I've had a garden, rabbi.

—See?

—You don't leave the plants in there forever. You pull them out by their roots. And then replant something new every season.

—Your argument precludes the possibility of perennials? Perhaps you fail to understand even the basic meaning of faith after all these years.

—Do I?

—What do you want? Belief in God only in joy? Without pain? Without anguish? You of all people should know. You cannot cheat suffering.

—Me? Of all people?

—Your father suffered a terrible illness, and he lost his ability to speak. Did he not?

—I don't think you like that I have a choice.

—Then you fail to divine the purpose of faith. A Jew's faith allows him to experience despair, despair in the face of life. To accept despair, and continue living in the presence of God. To prize deeds. *Teshuva, tefillah, tzedekah.* This is an element of affirmation expected of every Jew.

—My father's stroke is one of God's miracles?

—We survive by our faith. Let's not insult the suffering.

—It would be an insult to my suffering father to accept your argument.

—For all who suffered before us, you are responsible to be faithful.

—Who is going to punish me? If I'm not?

—We must continue to suffer as our ancestors suffered, and that is where our faith comes from. You must do the thing that ought to be done, when it ought to be done, as it ought to be done, whether you want to do it or not, the rabbi said, addressing the room in short, harsh bursts, like a prosecutor.

—And the children who died in the concentration camps? Were they responsible too?

Across the open chapel, a silence took hold. Hands rose up to cover mouths like you see in photographs of disasters. Friedman shot me a look, unsure what he was hearing. Gail sought my attention with her eyes.

In our fashion, we'd been slamming a lot doors between us, the rabbi and me, for a long time, but still we were bound to each other. And whether or not I truly understood what I was doing, I was much in need of his respect for me, of which I assumed there was always a reservoir. That I hadn't assumed otherwise goes a long way toward illustrating why I was callow enough to expect nothing more than the usual banter for asking questions as we were trained to do in that place. Because in that moment, in the presence of all my friends, I wasn't looking for something mystical. I wasn't looking for a unifying version of divine meaning or a moment of clarity the way faith is sometimes understood. It made no difference whether you labelled yourself—here I mean, myself—a person of faith or a person without faith. The insufficiencies were equal. I knew the counter-argument, of course—that because a Jew's work toward faith is never finished you're not permitted to quit. And yet, I had felt ready for this moment. All those rehearsal debates I'd done in my head, while walking along the bayou. I could taste globs of spit in my mouth. But what happened next surprised me.

—Am I obligated to ask only certain kinds of questions? I said.

—You're rejecting Judaism? You don't recognize your role in defending against the eternal hostility to our fellow Jews?

—There are many ways to be a human being.

—Do you want us to admire you for that observation? Is that it?

—If I'm always suffering for myself and others, what difference would it make? I don't have to feel guilty.

—God will know you're suffering. God is showing you how to be this way even now. "The Lord is good to all, and his tender mercies are over all his works." I tell you this for your own good. This subjectivity. It is not something you play around with.

—"The Lord is good to all, and his tender mercies are over all his works" doesn't mean I'm wicked.

—God is a miracle. God is in your eyes.

—You're in my eyes, I said, causing a new pain to spread between us.

—This is an insult to the very children you spoke of who died in the Shoah. Don't you feel any responsibility? Son, I've known you since you were in nursery school, since *Beth Hayeled*, since you were three years old. Going to wander the entire world the way you used to wander out of class? Is that it? You want to be provocative? Is that it? You want to be outrageous? Insulting? The wicked son? Let me tell you, this kind of thinking of yours is an offense. "The fool hath said in his heart, there is no God. Heal us, God, and we will be healed!" What do you need? Proof? A miracle?

—What proof would a silent God offer?

—If you believe in God, God exists.

—But if God doesn't exist, then what is the urgency of belief and rituals and all the rest? And the celebration of being victims all the time? We're the Six Day War champs. But, hey,

Bub, don't forget, you're a victim. You were chosen for it.

—Let me tell you something. You, all of you. You have not witnessed the real world. It has not grabbed you by the neck and pushed you to the ground so that God, as he does during *Pesach*, will say, "I have seen the affliction of My People that are in Egypt, and I have heard their cry and know their pains." Your kind of thinking leads to disaster, he shouted, and the air in the room seemed to rupture.

—God is going to make the pain a better pain? I guess we all have a choice. If there's no delight, what is there to treasure?

—The words are, *V'atah-im-sh'mo teeshmu-b'kolee ooshmartem et-breetee-v'yitem lee-s'gulah meekal-haahmim.* "If ye will hearken unto My voice, and keep My covenant, then ye shall be Mine own treasure from among all peoples." Mine. Own. Treasure. When you were speaking of treasure, those are the words you're looking for. That's enough. You are who you are.

—Chosen means choosing back. Right? It's not like we're stuffed dolls in a toy bin.

—You know what you want for yourself? Do you? You know what you want? To be no one? Is that it? You want to be from nowhere? You're an exception? Ladies and gentlemen, everybody, faith is like dry land. Faith is where you rest from the storms of life, he said and shuffled through his papers to find the exercise he wanted to pass out.

—Not a faith I'd want.

—Beg your pardon.

—Faith is a boat on the sea, in the fog, in the dark. Same as no faith. You still have to steer the boat, rabbi.

—So you just want to set sail? Is that it? Well, then. Go. Leave. Get out. You're out.

I did nothing at first, while he stood with his hand in his trousers, looking down at his shoes, waiting. I stood and slipped my books into my knapsack. The chapel was silent, but for a soft voice, Gail Gerber's, saying my name.

Riding my bicycle home under the hot sun that morning, I felt fully declared, as if I might no longer be immersed in the Jewish dirt of my existence, or a member of its Texas society.

For days there'd been a series of heavy thunderstorms, unusual for spring, and I pedaled past curbs with water-soaked debris—a desk with no drawers, couches and chairs, side table, a sink, insulation, torn-out lathe. The flooding was already receding, with small lakes standing near street corners, and fallen trees splayed across lawns, ripped out at the roots, gutters collapsed in driveways.

When I came to Meyerland Park, I stopped in the open ball field. There were people sitting on a blanket in the grass, and one of them appeared to be playing a wind instrument like a recorder. I wanted to get closer but didn't, and instead walked over to one of the black rubber swings and sat down, and pushed back and forth, my feet scraping the dirt. The long chains creaked. The grass trembled and swayed. After a while I found shade under a small tree and waited there. I couldn't make out the music anymore. Behind me two boys were playing tennis, facing each other across the net, striking the yellow ball with grunting rallies. Their deliberate movements cast shadows across the court.

How uneventfully that morning had begun. I had been sitting in the synagogue with my friends, the windows clear, skies slowly rising, cloud by glowing cloud. By the time I walked out I had staked a position that religion was a lie, and Judaism offensive. During the first part of the bike ride toward home, I realized I had seldom felt so untroubled. Under the bright Jewish skies of Texas with the clouds bursting in widening gaps, I was at last a renegade. It felt radiant to be in the hot air. The crevices of my spirit smoothed out.

I stood to go home, kicked the bike in place, but didn't get on.

Bending my head over the seat like I was going to be sick, I suddenly felt disgraced, disgusted. At first I thought if I could hide what had happened, grind it down to where it couldn't be found, I might be able to leave my house for the synagogue each week for class but then hide and not show up. Immediately I could see how ridiculous this thinking was. I'd hide and just not tell anyone? What was that about? The charade would be a miserable undertaking. It wasn't any use to hide. I had to find what was right, and yet I knew I had found what was right. Even if I did turn back, I knew I wouldn't get clear of what now I understood my life to mean to me.

I was in trouble.

The people sitting in the grass began to play their recorder again. The music trembled on a breeze. There was no way to shove all that I had said to the rabbi out of my head. As much out of stubbornness as anything else, as much out of a feeling that by being kicked out I had got what I wanted, I understood simply that I was in this new life now for good.

When I think of all that now, after so many years, I wonder if it's possible for others to make sense of it. One disastrous argument, and that changes everything?

Is it the same for trying to interpret one's whole history? Or the history of a home? After you've left it? As you would the rings of years of a severed tree trunk? Can you see its scars? Hear its little moments of grace and struggle, sufferings and triumphs, sickness, good fortune, the intrusions withstood, floods survived? Can you hear the talking and pleading and sobbing over the state of the nation, devotion to children, affection for the elderly or newlyweds, catching a cold, or beating an egg?

Perhaps that's the sense of longing I'm talking about, where home is like a call, and in that call is your recognition that you have a longing in the first place. The call is a summons. You are alert to it. Living day to day through the hard hours in whatever home you are in, however far away, means always responding to the call. You can be called at anytime, from anywhere. Sometimes you recognize in the call, too, a kind of ringing, like a buoy bell. Other times you don't recognize the call or refuse it. Still other times the call is mysterious, difficult to perceive, even terrifying. No matter, the call keeps coming. Out of your longing to respond, you live to discover what's been lost, as if you're standing uneasily before your own life, saying, I just want to be nothing except what I am, flowing just as I am. Flowing, and flown.

Mother had her eyes down so that her anger became more and more dense. The living room felt murky in the cell of silence she was creating around us, as if spinning all of history into a forgotten gap in time, as if to acknowledge that if one of us began talking, the earth at that moment might jerk off its axis.

—A Jew doesn't have to live for faith. You, my dear son, have never let on at any time that being Jewish makes you unhappy. I feel I don't know you anymore. You aren't the son I know. Don't close your face up like a steel trap. You're going to hear what I have to say. You never talked about how you feel. Not once did you so much as hint. Not a single time did you say, Mother, I need to share some things with you. Never, nada, not. Never saying a word to me. Whether you like it or not, you make me feel like some kind of ogre, unfeeling, unthinking, uncaring, unloving. This is a terrible thing you've done. Are you listening to me? Mother said.

—Yes.

—No matter what I say, you won't like it. We all have our reasons for why we do things and how we feel about events. I'm not going to mince words about how I feel and why. As your grandfather says, however many days the good Lord gives me, I'll take them. But this is a day I wish I never had. I'd like to give that rabbi a piece of my mind. I do not like what happened today and will probably always remain unhappy about the circumstances and behavior that led you to do this. Even if you think the rabbi was foolish, you'll have to get over your anger towards him. That's just the way it is, that's just the way I feel, and, frankly, I have a legitimate right to those feelings. I blame all this on that rabbi. And you and your father and brothers aren't much better. I've been treated badly by all of you for years, not a kind word from any of you. I'm surprised I haven't had a nervous breakdown. I had already made plans to run away and leave everything behind before your father became ill. I know you didn't know that. But it's true.

Mother looked away. Her eyes small and clear. I felt flush, unbalanced, unaccustomed to my new self, wondering how to adapt to this new attack.

I was remembering something right then. Immediately after the start of the Yom Kippur War, in 1973, when I was nine years old, petition booths sprang up all over Meyerland asking the Nixon administration to continue its support of Israel, and a blood donation site was set up in Braeswood Square. I'd joined with my friends, the very ones I'd just left behind for good in that chapel, to take up a collection after school. We knocked on hundreds of doors in the hot afternoons, bounding up and down the sidewalks.

When someone opened the door I started talking right away, working through the riff I'd rehearsed with my mother. I said, you're aware of the war in Israel now, right? I've come today to ask for your help. You can do something important and decisive right now today. You can buy Israel bonds and help Israel in its hour of need. Make your check payable directly to the State of Israel. Please. Help us. You'll be able to say you didn't just read the news and worry. My class will be sending money directly to the government of Israel.

As one neighbor after another had me wait on the porch to get a checkbook, I could feel the air-conditioning whisk through the crack in the opened door. House by house I went, ringing the doorbells, making my pitch, and sliding the checks into a yellow envelope. The small act of going door to door to raise a few hundred dollars accrued something glorious deep into my body.

A few days later I received a hand-written letter from my grandfather in the mail that read, "When I was new in this country, I lived in a small Iowa town. I worked a scrap wagon and everywhere I went it was a struggle. I was nobody. Now I have a desk and people come to me. Now I am respected. To me, Israel is like that desk—a symbol of the respect we as a people have earned. When I was in Israel recently, I felt as I have felt nowhere else in any corner of the world. I was a Jew, yes, but more than that I felt I was a part of all mankind. Even in the United States with all our freedom, I have never felt such a complete sense of belonging. Your mother tells me you are going house to house and raising money for our fellow Jews. Enclosed is a check. You're a good boy. Love, Grandpa Joe."

—After twenty-two years of motherhood, you'd think I could just accept things as they are and go on about my own business. At this stage, I can't change, and after forty-six years of my life, I'm not going to abandon what I believe in. Judaism isn't only about faith. Do the right thing, and God will take care of the rest. I didn't send you to Jewish Day School for you to pretend you don't understand what's going on here. You'll have to apologize. And don't fake it. I've learned the hard way, fool me once, no second chance. I no longer believe in ideal anything.

She disappeared into the kitchen, and left me to sit alone in the living room. The afternoon light cast a low wave over the floors and Mother's bookshelves, a mixture of popular novels, history, and politics. There was nothing on Southern culture on those shelves. Not even a cookbook. Cornpone, she called it. There was one shelf that held her favorite textbooks from college, while the others were lined with books on Judaism. Things like Abba Eban's *My People. The Rise and Fall of the Third Reich. The New Israelis. The Wisdom of Israel. The Illustrated Atlas of Jewish Civilization. Middle East Dilemmas. Jews in Minnesota. Dakota Diaspora. My Rabbi Doesn't Make House Calls. Mazel Tov—You're Middle-Aged.*

Stories of Shalom Aleichem. Jewish Woman in America. Ess, Ess, Mein Kindt. Night. Dawn.

Some time later we resumed talking in the kitchen, while she cooked dinner, although she seemed to forget what she was supposed to do with the pan of raw chicken thighs in her hand.

—What fool rabbi argues with his student and kicks him out? Another rabbi would have found a thousand ways to keep you in class.

—It doesn't matter.

—Judaism is not a religion based on theology. It's not about doctrines. What you don't understand is that religious acts and practices establish a pattern of Jewish life. That's it.

—Yeah, but it's pretty evident, isn't it, that the practices are tethered to faith, expressions of faith in the all-encompassing sovereignty of God. Halakhah isn't just some recommended set of guidelines. It's the final authority, I said, speaking about the Jewish Code.

—There are only two principles you need to know. Yes, God's sovereignty is one, but more important, is the sacredness of every individual. You might start by acquainting yourself with the Ten Commandments, especially the fifth. Do you know that one?

—Yes.

—Do you?

—To honor thy father and mother.

—Give that one a try. You don't like the first principle, fine. You won't be the only Jew who doesn't believe in God. Focus on the second one.

—Is it a buffet? Follow the Fifth Commandment? But not the first two? I am the Lord your God who brought you out of bondage, out of the land of Egypt, into the land of Meyerland. Thou shalt have no other Gods before me. You're the one saying it's multiple choice.

—Then don't forget the Fourth Commandment, she said, still holding the chicken pan.

—Are there any days of human existence Halakhah doesn't have a rule about?

—Halakhah offers guidance.

—Really? Every aspect of life is subject to it. How to conduct business. Check. How to interact socially. Check. How to entertain. Check. How you make art, how you eat, how you have sex. Check, check, check. All are under one Jewish prism. One Jewish prison.

—You think that's funny? I don't have patience right now for your little wordplays. The only reason that a Jew needs for the observance of any of the commandments, whatever you want to call them, is that they reflect the will of God.

—Am I servant of the Lord?

—A Jewish person tries to carry them out. Yes, as a duty. Not having faith has never stopped a Jew from trying to understand the reasons for the various laws and commandments.

I couldn't have articulated it, in the kitchen, in that house, in the fading evening light, when I was seventeen, that I did understand, with every atom of my body, that, when faithfully observed, Jewish religion is itself life. But, still, I was intent. I had to forsake it, to disavow, relinquish, quit, and, finally, simply to retire from the authority and the jurisdiction of the Torah and Halakhah.

Which meant I had to leave Texas.

—Don't worry about it. I'll be fine, I said finally, but that was the kind of talk, I knew, made my mother livid.

—You were rude to the rabbi. I am certain of that. I know how you get. You always think you're one step ahead. Always. When I die, don't stand silently at my grave. At my funeral I better hear you saying Kaddish. And not mumbling. If you're not going to enunciate, don't bother coming to my funeral.

The pan of raw chicken slumped on the counter. The pieces had rolled to one side. She walked out of the kitchen into her room, closing the door behind her.

The rest of the evening I felt a fear deepening in my mother's presence. We moved around each other like people sweeping the floors, laboriously deliberate. Whenever I walked into one room or another, I felt I could see her out of the corner of my eye. When I walked into the den, I caught a glimpse of something outside like light through the window, like a car driving past the house. But when I looked, nothing.

Finally I went to my room, remorseless, lying on the bed, looking up at the ceiling, wondering what I was going to do now that I had determined I was going to live differently, besmirched, blind with my coherence and self-confidence, ruthlessly shrinking from nothing.

Near midnight Mother came to the edge of my bedroom in her housecoat and slippers, and stood in the threshold of the open door. She stood with her arms crossed as if my presence made her feel hemmed in. She must have been worried that my decision would become normal and therefore dangerous—at the same time, she must have assumed that eventually I'd relent, that one day, even if I held firm for some years, the suppleness of my decision would overtake my head and arms, then my shoulders and legs, and, not knowing what else to do, I'd come walking toward home, toward her, as if out of a mirage, and while she'd barely believe what she was seeing, I'd have returned at last, as if across a windy desert. The lost son come home. We'd forget any of this had ever happened and sit down to Shabbat dinner of chicken and peas and potatoes like a promise long kept, and attend evening services, and everything would go back to being what it was.

—You are in danger of becoming a lonely person, abandoning your heritage, disappointing your friends. I don't even want to begin to think what this will do to your grandfather.

—Even the Zionists wanted to flee Jewish life in Europe. A little hand in hand, you might say, I said.

—The Zionists? Now what are you talking about? What do Zionists have to do with you?

—They sure ditched Yiddish fast enough once they got Israel going. Didn't they? Yiddish, no. Nukes, yes.

—I don't understand what you're even talking about.

—We're told to feel guilty for leaving Jews behind in Europe because of the Holocaust. We're told to glorify Israel, if not the Holocaust itself.

—Don't start.

—We're told we're always a day away from being victims again, and yet also that Israel is the mightiest little engine that could of a nation the world has ever seen. The obligations are endless.

—What are you talking about? This is why you don't want to study Torah or practice Judaism? The Zionists? Don't pull that on me. Do you even know the difference between Judaism and Zionism?

—I do.

—I'm not so sure.

—One's a religion, a people. The other is a political movement. It's not rocket science, I said.

—You're going to be nothing but heartache. Just waltzing out into the world looking for ways to give me grief. There's no one like my son to make me feel like a complete failure as a mother.

—That's not true, about failure. The Old Testament says not to hold a grudge anyway, I said.

—Do not refer to Hebrew Scripture as the Old Testament, she said, leaning against the door, staring at the floor.

—It's not incorrect.

—I'm not accusing you of being incorrect. Only of using the wrong words. The earliest Jews created Hebrew Scripture out of their lives.

—But the rest of us are supposed to create our lives out of those scriptures. It's backwards. It's pretend. It's make-believe. Anyway, don't worry about it, I said, trying to get the last word in, as if I was trying to tell her something about life she didn't know.

That sparked a slightly caustic laugh from her, and I knew right then, looking at her in her housecoat looking terribly, terribly sad, appearing as if not only her but all of Jewry was capriciously sullied and put at risk by my incomprehensible betrayal, that we would be having this row for decades to come, destined to walk up and down this same street, over and over, around the corner and up the next one, this long, empty street, bypassing all the shops, crossing to walk up the other side, turning the corner, going to the next street, walking down that one. But never arriving anywhere.

I always felt I won the quarrel with the rabbi, in part because I was dismissed.

I left, as instructed. I left what I took to be the insularity, the monotony, and the rectitude of Meyerland. I left in order to think about anything else but all that, to endure any other aspects of life, to go anywhere else. I left not because I didn't have community, or love, or a home. Not because I thought of faith as some fact, some arrival, some certainty the way people do when they use the word faith sometimes. I didn't have faith in faith, is what it was. Because I didn't have faith in any of it—faith in the rituals to praise God, in the possibility of God, in Torah as the fullness of life, nor recovering any of that in the future, and the belonging that went with it.

I recognize that for some, all that possibility is the allure. But that's what I was repudiating.

Over time, like a lot of people, I've become a person who views religion as a machinery of thought, and like any machinery it can be used for noble callings and it can be used for wicked ones. I've become a person who is not prepared to live under the insinuation that the universe is designed with human beings in mind—or worse, that there is a heavenly plan into which everyone fits, whether they want to or not, or know it or not. A secularist like me is comfortable with uncertainty, curiosity, inquiry, trial and error. In the end I simply prefer my ignorance to the other guy's dogma.

And yet, if home is the location of our most essential

relationships and most formative moments, then our stories of home are worthy of reflection as we piece together the events of our lives. Our personal narratives are a means to maintain some sort of continuity of consciousness.

I have lived in over a dozen houses or apartments since I left Texas, perhaps been a different person in each one, and yet the memory of my response to my mother's feelings about the quarrel that night is one of the pillars I associate with home. Texas may not be the center of my physical universe, but it is the center of my cognitive one. I wanted to leave Meyerland to conquer a different world, with all its perils and rewards, because of a powerful, evolutionary desire to feel, paradoxically, at home.

Later on, when my life was more my own, I would look back on that spring day like a trophy on the mantel, a Texas souvenir.

Of course, I was aware of what my actions meant. I knew the historic American Jewish narrative: that, since the founding of the republic, Jews have felt at home in America more easily than we could anywhere else in the history of the world, that methods of social exclusion did not diminish Jewish insistence that America was a better place than others where Jews had lived, that economic opportunity, tied to legal safeguards, nourished Jews's patriotism in America, that Jews volunteered to fight and die for their new country, that in the aftermath of the Second World War, in the face of the genocide of European Jewry, American Jews confronted the luck of their geography and held firm to the notion that, unlike in other countries, they could use civic, economic, and intellectual mechanisms to protect themselves, that when American Jews recognized, by mid-twentieth century, that they had more power than other minority groups, Jews became activists in the civil rights movement and the women's movement and progressive causes.

In Texas I was a product of all that, as well as of the sentiment, often expressed during my boyhood, that since the founding of modern Israel in 1948 Jews were likely to lose more people in America through assimilation—what the Nazis couldn't achieve, American Jews, through intermarriage, would achieve in the dark nights of their bedrooms.

It's a daunting narrative.

Going to bed that night, after the row with my mother, and after the quarrel with the rabbi, I felt that familiar melancholy, as Shelly Rose had seen that day under the leafy trees of Lymbar Drive, until I recognized that very feeling was the root of my desire. I felt jubilant. I felt liberated from the persistent sensation and weight and agitation. True, it didn't take much to crack the illusion of separation, to bring me back to my excruciating history.

Over time, I realized I simply had nothing to lose, no more or less than what we all lose anyway.

I learned from that experience that a high level of comfort with deliberate uncertainty is of my skin, in my eyes and ears, on my tongue. It's the very thing that makes me me. It's one of the things that makes life livable. Perpetual uncertainty, the not knowing what comes next.

IN THE VALLEY OF THE GHOSTS

Horizon

And the city stood in its brightness when years later I returned,
My face covered with a coat though now no one was left
Of those who could have remembered my debts never paid,
My shames not forever, base deeds to be forgiven.

            —Czeslaw Milosz

When it comes down to it, Milosz's imaginary return from exile offers us a vision of alarmed disorientation, and not so much a close encounter with a posthumous life. Put another way, it demonstrates there are many ways to be alive with curiosity and defiance, even as the past spares nothing. It's impossible to prepare for it, and it's probably a merciful thing that shame is so hard to describe, or the place where the shame occurred, especially when, as in my story, it's wrapped up with what I always took to be my triumph.

Recently, perhaps mercifully, I was having trouble summoning even that part of the memory about how I felt during those lacerating years. I began to wonder if going home after all this time—to reacquaint myself with the wide open streets and the muggy air and to feel the valor and swagger of what is, and always is, Texas—might permit me to appreciate the old passageways without shattering my imagination. I had feared, if that's the word, that I might have become too successful—I don't know how to put this—at reinventing my own consciousness.

So it was—after the Memorial Day flood and the Tax Day flood, but before Hurricane Harvey—when the last of the year's heat was dwindling, I flew to Texas and arrived in

Meyerland after nearly forty years to wander around the streets in the hope of unravelling a knot.

To some extent, I discovered what I was looking for, beginning with the strange joy of standing again under Houston's bulbous clouds and seeing the sand and dirt of Chimney Rock Road and Rice Avenue, the straightaways of North Braeswood and South Braeswood that are so long they seem to die before they end, idle lawns and forgotten debris, the freeway overpass, receding strip malls, and noticing crevices between the brick houses so lonely only a shadow can rest there.

It was a stone blue day, bright clouds sloshing in the distance, when I stepped out of the car where I parked behind Braeswood Square, near my old house, to walk to the corner of Chimney Rock Road and North Braeswood. Like magnetic filings the cars came and went, some with grime on their wheels, others gleaming from a nearby car wash with dapples of water beading on the windows. The people in the cars that waited at the red light—all of them separate from each other, with patches of sunlight filtering in over their faces and across the seats—were silent. The toot of a horn could be heard in the distance. All of which made me feel as if I was a lone drifter, the last survivor of my own life.

When the light changed, I crossed North Braeswood and stepped onto the asphalt trail along the bayou, turning west toward the footbridge to the Jewish Community Center.

Save for the thick spongy grass, there was not much to be seen in every direction but flat ground and the long horizon. At the water's edge four white birds tiptoed and drank from the water, and wood debris caught in the center caused a small rapids to form. There were dozens of newly planted trees. Brown and yellow butterflies. A seagull flying east. At my feet were dead patches of grass from recent flooding, and across North Braeswood were the Nob Hill Apartments' NOW LEASING banners and Texas flags. I gently kicked at an ant hill. Hundreds of ants scurried. A long honk in the distance. Joggers cruised by. Mothers with strollers. An elderly couple in tennis shoes walking without haste and talking loudly about the grandchildren. What tiny flowers were here through the exaggerated heat of spring and summer were sparse. Stiff flax and dayflowers crowded the ridge above the steep slope where swallows treaded the air like late falling leaves. A spiny turtle submerged in the water was paddling sideways. Another turtle came up beside it. The sky seemed worn out even in its blueness.

I looked ahead and was comforted by the windy distance. Show me that horizon, I said out loud as I walked under the winnowed sky, the span tempting me to explore further, to conceive its unreadable line that seemed to offer choices with its basic curve and sensation of endings.

I love to watch a horizon, and, it seems, it watches me too. Beyond every horizon lie the hauntings of the next one, all those places that hide the sensuous, where sky and land mark an impression. The sight-lines shift a little, offering a physical thrill with how intensely factual it is. I must have learned that growing up here, when I'd walk toward this horizon sensing it waiting up ahead like a distant future. Perhaps there is some old longing in my desire for horizons, longing for their atmosphere and silence that holds me in devotion—even the smallest window can offer a view like an unmarked secret.

Underfoot there was the clicking of crickets. Overhead, ocean liners of clouds passed, opening up wakes of blue sky. A siren cut south toward Willowbend Boulevard. The sweet aroma of smoke from the Hickory BBQ where I imagined the juke box was playing Ronnie Milsap's "Almost Like a Song" or Buck Owens's "Open Up Your Heart and Let My Love Come In."

A flock of swallows broke into two squadrons, one to the east, the other to the west. Birds dipped behind Braeswood Square, returned over the water and moved south above Chimney Rock Road, heading through hidden places under the clouds. Everywhere was the monotonous, spongy grass and the stink of the bayou's water. Humidity clinging to my shirt. On the other side of the bayou a pony-tailed man was netting a long silver fish.

My itinerary was to walk past the footbridge that crossed the bayou to the Jewish Community Center, walk over to Temple Beth Israel, then north to Herod Elementary School, then circle east, time permitting, to Johnston Junior High, split off toward Godwin Park and over again to the footpath above the bayou at Rice Avenue, where I'd walk through Meyerland Park to get to Loch Lomond outside my old house. Finally I'd return to the rental car parked outside the Stop N' Go. At the end of the day I had an appointment to enter Beth Yeshurun—permission was required to get past the armed guard outside the building. It was to be the first time I'd been inside the shul in nearly forty years, since the day of the quarrel.

For my walk, I wanted to take in the atmosphere, is all.

Would I still feel the sensation that nothing felt lonelier than walking above Brays Bayou? Would walking along the bayou, as if crossing a psychic valley, allow me to hear the many voices of the past speaking at once? Would I still be in awe of my exposure to the huge sky? Would that also, strangely, feel pleasing to me?

No sharp hillsides would ever appear. No ridges or forests of towering trees such as there are where I live in Oregon, and with them the explorable secrets in their enclosed density. The walk was wide open and flat, patches of sky familiar as the teeth in my own head. What overtook my mind was the bayou's water, running slow and low, until the rains come when it can quickly rise and overflow the banks.

There was flooding in Brays Bayou as far back as the 1840s with bridges leading into the small city submerged under water from thunderstorms. The historic reports of East Texas floods are eerily repetitive. In 1900, a catastrophic hurricane hit Galveston. A third of the city was destroyed. Over six thousand people died. A tropical storm landed near Corpus Christi in South Texas in 1919, moved up the coast and brought seven inches of rain over Houston with Brays Bayou's gage height

rising to fifty-six feet, making it one of the hardest hit water-
ways. Small boats were the only transportation for a week.
In October 1949 ten inches of rain fell in twenty four hours
causing Brays Bayou to run over its banks, and some hundred
homes were flooded. Ten years later, another hundred homes
flooded in seven inches of rainfall in just two hours. From the
nineteen seventies to the early nineteen eighties, the names of
Texas hurricanes and tropical storms are like a yearbook of
high water and damaged lives: Celia, Felice, Edith, Delia, and
Carmen. Anita, Amelia, and Claudette. Alan, Norma, Alicia,
and Barry. Storm water from 1989's Hurricane Allison caused a
quarter of the houses to be flooded.

Tropical storms were so common when I was a boy,
strangely routine, that I often just went to bed when the
power went out and slept through them, much to Mother's
consternation, especially after it was just the two of us living
together. Vigilance is needed, she said once, as she stood in the
dark hallway outside my door during one nighttime hurricane.
I straggled to the kitchen in my teenage body, the windows
stretched hard in their sashes and frames, whining against the
wind, a steady jangling of rain against the shingles, a short
candle flickering in the center of the oval kitchen table, and
we resumed gin rummy with the cards casting long rectangular
shadows.

I stepped away from the bayou and dipped into a side street,
walking among a loose scattering of houses. There was an
odd grandeur about them left standing empty from the recent
floods. Piled along the curbs were soggy couches and mat-
tresses, curtain rods, wall hangings, tile and yard equipment
once stored in garages. I saw plastic toys and cedar chests. A
stand-up piano. Matching ceramic lamps. Stained snapshots.
Rolled-up rugs. A baseball mitt. An urn. There were bras-
sieres and socks abandoned in the dried-out streets. I imagined
they'd floated in the receding water for days, like cuttings of
food backed up in a sink.

I imagined how, after those terrible floods, the sky cleared, the lawns gleamed with large puddles while the neighborhood exhaled a little joy in the humid air under puffy clouds.

On Friday nights, after big storms, when I lived here, with streets still half-flooded, women from the Sisterhood, from the various congregations, walked up driveway after driveway to people's homes, several hundred homes, delivering challahs despite their own houses being flooded.

Once these mid-century modern houses had stood proud-ly. The rooms were places of hospitality and festivities, filled with the voices of those the floods had chased away. Water-logged now, they were pillars of bricks waiting to fall down. Empty swimming pools stained with green scum and gardens overgrown with weeds. How well I knew their mute language. They seemed deeply to embody what I felt—Meyerland had become like a mourner, and I was a visitor, something of a ruin myself.

Near Godwin Park, the damage from the flooding was im-possible to ignore.

Where I expected to find familiar houses were just windy patches of grass. An elevated mansion was built in the next lot over to replace what I remembered was a modest ranch house. Next to that were several boarded houses. Here, a house was demolished, standing half-upright like a fallen tree. Across the street were one, two, three grassy lots in a row—that was where Lauren Reiter's house used to be. Wasn't it? All that was left was a plot of dirt. Remaining houses were up for sale.

I began to imagine that every week some new bankruptcy was filed. With the expectation from catastrophic climate change that future storms will be more frequent and severe on the Gulf Coast, there appeared no sign of an end to what I felt must be encroaching anxiety. I was unprepared for the feeling of heartbreak that took hold of me. It's one thing to read about how the floods ruined homes and displaced people's lives after the devastation and quite another to walk, on a mild sunny day, past scores of FOR SALE signs. It was difficult to imagine the discussions a family might have had about whether to stay, or the concerns of the grandmother who lives in the spare room and says one morning, as the parents leave the house to walk the children to school and then drive to work, we should appreciate what we have and be satisfied with good enough.

As the air brightened, I felt a lonely tranquility. These were not streets where you wander past crowds of pedestrians coasting both ways on the narrow sidewalks. No sidewalk trade as you see in the streets of New York or Paris, folding tables with bootleg CDs and used paperbacks. No immigrant merchants selling soap or incense, or small blue bottles of lotions or perfume. Few people passing by at all to greet you with a look of the eye, returning a nod. You would never see much less hear the horns of a taxicab.

A black gentleman, with an unlit cigar in his mouth, hurried across the street, house to house, delivering free copies of the *Southwest News*. I waved him down. There was an article on a new wellness program moving into the space vacated by the Levy Funeral Home. A forty-fifth reunion at Bellaire High, where I'd gone to high school. A noted author speaking at the Houston Holocaust Museum. Photographs of flappers in sequins, pearls, and headbands, and men in zoot suits and fedoras, for the Houston branch of the National Council of Jewish Women's 1920s-themed gala. Advertisements for upholstery, brick repair, flooring replacement.

I took delight in the remaining, older brick houses, strung out intermittently in a straight line on some streets, divided by narrow driveways and two-car garages. I recognized all those houses and had been inside a lot of them—before school or after school or for sleepovers. Where gardens brightened with autumn flowers, there was a smell of pine. Damp piles of leaves shoved against white fences. Blue fire hydrants. Texas flags. Political signs around which the wind slowed. A red tricycle abandoned in a front lawn. On one street corner there was a faded blue Hanukah banner still up from last year and, rooted in the lawn, peeling white Adirondack chairs. A siren in the distance.

Most of the Jewish families living here, I knew, had not themselves emigrated from far-off crossroads in Eastern Europe to reach the refuge of these cul-de-sacs. Still, some had arrived from the Soviet Union in the 1970s or Ethiopia in the 1980s. It was typical of Houston to welcome new arrivals. The city took in two hundred thousand Vietnamese refugees in the 1970s. After Hurricane Katrina, Houston took in a quarter of a million evacuees. As many as forty thousand people stayed. I've read Houston resettles twenty-five of every thousand refugees from across the world through programs of the United Nations—that's more than any other city in America, and more than most countries.

M aking my way past Contour Street and circuitously over to Queensloch, past Rutherglen, all of a sudden into my head came a melody. It curved softly from impulse to a breezy gentleness. To my astonishment I found myself singing the refrain fluently, as if the distant past was emerging in the form of an odd numbness. No matter which way I tried to shift my mind from the melody—and, failing that, tried to sift through the words—I kept coming back to the opening verse.

I wasn't at all confused, and sang softly.

> *Ashrei-yosh-vay-vay-techa od-ye-halelu-lah-se-lah*
> *Ashrei-ha-am-sheh-ca-chah-lo ash-ram-ha-am-*
> *sheh-ashem-elo-hav.*

It was *Ashrei*, the prayer that expresses the covenant between Jews and God as a pathway to eternity. In nearly two dozen verses, *Ashrei* holds the code of Jewish thought. It shows the faithful the essence of the relationship between God and human beings, said twice in the morning service and once in the afternoon as fanfare. Anyone who says *Ashrei* three times a day, who says it with earnest faith after deep study, who says it to discover humility in the greatness of God, is guaranteed a place in the world to come and the forgiveness of their sins. Generations can be heard speaking to each other in *Ashrei*. The pious no more than the sinful. To inherit eternity is the reward for fulfillment of this one commandment. This call to praise joy. To praise God.

In no time, I was overcome with old repudiations.

Did one think I couldn't find joy without this one prayer? Was joy to be denied to me? Who is trying to keep that secret from me and entice me with an eternal prize? If God is good to all, I thought, and his tender mercies are over all his works, as *Ashrei* says, why is it necessary to always bless his name with such incessant devotion for doing what God already does? If God could heal a blind man, why not heal blindness? With so much prayer, why so few results? *Ashrei* or no, death is coming.

Gamely, I offered the familiar rabbinical rejoinders, just as I had as a teenager walking on this very footpath. You're disloyal. You have no conscience. Responsibility means nothing to you. Obligation means nothing to you. Decency, conduct, moral code, suffering, grit, your family—you think it's all expendable. You think you're untouchable. Why so petty? So vengeful? Unforgiving? Are we that distasteful you have to vilify us? Do you have such contempt for your own life? Look, came another voice in my head, you may not understand now, but later after you lose things in life, you'll get it.

No comfort in that. Is there? As if being told none of this is true but never mind that. Being told, we know this is a misrepresentation of humankind, but follow it anyway. Not just that God exists but that God built this whole world for us, here and in the world to come.

"The eyes of the people look to you, and you give them food in due season," says *Ashrei*, "Open your divine hands and satisfy every living thing with your favor."

I stopped, bent forward, and another set of melodies came into my head, from the soundtrack to *Fiddler on the Roof* which used to play in so many of the houses on these streets when I was growing up. The eight-track cassettes spooling out all those sentimental Broadway melodies. Even as a boy, I used to feel those songs were creepily at odds with my grandfather's stories, not about how he had to tear himself away from shtetl life, or wishing he could return to Cherniostrov with a show tune on his lips, but that life there was menacing, poverty-stricken, and best forgotten. It wasn't that I was unaware of anti-Semitism when I was very young. It's just that growing up Jewish in Texas during the Cold War felt like a perfectly normal way of growing up American. The two seemed nearly indistinguishable. Much of the confidence with which we Jewish kids in Meyerland seized our sense of freedom—the basic assumption that one American was entitled to no less than any other American, that one should be excluded from nothing—came from our trust in belonging and believing in the unlimited opportunities in the America in which we lived.

Then, without warning, I thought of Velvet, my old dog, in the utility room gulping water, lapping it, her tags jingling around her neck, and then she pushes through the door into my room, rolls over on her brown side, curls her body and tucks her nose into a flank until she's dozing blissfully.

I thought of her when she was getting older, sleeping more deeply than she used to, slower to stand, her breathing labored. Sometimes I'd lay down next to her on the carpeted floor and pat her fur, scratching underneath her gray chin. She was warm against my body, my chest to her ribs, as if we were indistinguishable from each other. The day my father came home from the hospital, the year I was twelve, she never left my side. Something strange happened that day. I'll never forget. Gulls had landed in the front yard, far from sea. Wings closed tight, walking in random shapes, they made a curious sight so many of them in the lawn like a congregation of white dolls. Some quickly took to flight, flapping against the sky, or hovering to

settle down across the road. I went into my parents's room to
see if my father was all right, home now after three months in
the hospital. He'd been in there awhile, alone. By the time I got
down the hallway, I felt my spirit was soaked, a strange discon-
nection with him back in the house three months since that
first day in intensive care when the side of his mouth drooped
and his pupils were sluggish to react and he kept rubbing his
forehead with his left fist.

He was sleeping in a soft chair, with his feet on the ottoman,
a blanket over his legs. All the air in the room seemed unmoving, like water in a bowl. I thought maybe I should pull the
blanket up or shake his arm and suggest he get into bed, but
instead I sat on the blue carpet in the threshold of the door,
hugging my knees, with Velvet lying still beside me, breathing
hard, leaning her back against my feet. I watched the color in
my father's face change with each breath. His mouth was open,
breathing raggedly, the air entering him, and his silent mind.
I sat there and did nothing. Kept my own breath quiet. Just
then he woke up in the chair, unaware that I was on the floor,
reached across his unshaved face with his hand and rubbed his
mouth, coughed and cleared his throat hard. He saw me looking at him, squinted his blue eyes, put his palms together the
way people do when they're saying a prayer, and touched the
back of his hands to one cheek.

Next day I walked up the driveway from school and found
him sitting on the back step. Bad hurting, he said, mangling the
words, before dropping Velvet's silver dog tags into my palm.

For weeks the house felt totally empty, as if beauty had
been interrupted. For a long time I would think about Velvet's
last moments alone at the veterinarian's office, her shifting
uneasiness around the interns, her black and gray face, looking
outward with her soft eyes, a last sharp brightness of living, the
edges of the room darkening to a blurriness she never knew before, before dipping her head, unmoving. I would try to get my
mind around the idea of what was now to be her long absence.
I dug a hole for her in my spirit, a hollow circle that she might

gather her soul into, and not feel abandoned even in death.

The bayou, *Ashrei*, Velvet.

Near the water opened up the sight of a broken shopping cart sunk in the mud. I was transfixed by the streaks of salt and the gray stains on the banks. A heron standing on the grass leapt downward, flapped twice, and flew along the top of the water toward the curved horizon in a beautiful easy pace, then wheeled, winging higher and higher above the wide trees, its feathers beating hard under the sky, until it flew toward the Loop and, at last, blended into the slender clouds drifting downtown.

My body was no more noticeable to anyone right then than mist is to a stone.

In all this churning emotion, in all this thrust and rebuff, the old verbal sparring and the way all of life was a non-stop debate came roaring back. Perhaps it would've been better not to have come home, where it's easier to miss the meanings, where not everything needs to be felt and noted, written and interpreted.

When it comes to what you think of as your true home, I suppose, childhood is one's proof of citizenship.

The thing about entering the past all alone is, it expects you to know more about it than it does. The past trusts you've thought deeply about the rhythms of what has happened to you. The sagacity of memory is that it's always nearby to offer direction and disposition, caution and counsel, cure and comfort.

And, rebuke.

What was I thinking I would find when I walked around these long streets and pondered how I left Texas as someone wrestling with the choices of growing up in an ethnic group, in possession of all that glorious disgust about all that conformity? It was the natural course of events for me, as an ambitious young man, to deny my birthright and rebel. To emerge as myself, as an individual in America in the 1980s, required destructiveness. Self-destructiveness, if that's what you want to call it.

After I left Texas in 1982, I had drifted on what I took to be light-sparkling waves of a new secular life. The ceremonies and occasions that had once marked time in my Jewish observance, like ports of call on the horizon, I passed by, my mouth filled with an acidic taste. It didn't take much work to forget that this autumn month brought the High Holidays or that spring month brought Passover, and I hadn't noticed at all, or that each Friday night, by not tending it, I violated the sabbath. Early on, after I set out from Texas, I determined to make myself solitary. I believed solitude could take me towards an otherwise unattainable experience of reality. Whether I was living in the remote hillsides of Vermont or at Ocean Beach in San Francisco, I felt flooded in my strangeness, amputated from everyone else, forging new commonplaces, and tending to the business of my existence in alien rooms.

Nearly forty years passed—I'd hardly crossed the border back into Meyerland in all that time. What's more, had hardly wanted to because I always saw myself as feeling endangered by the insularity of my upbringing, the people, the heritage, and the cause. Seeking a new kind of American grist, volunteering for displacement, like an insurgent, I overturned my Texas existence. For my life's meaning, I ditched the power of one kind of literature for another—the poetry of Abraham's Hebron and Moses' Mount Horeb and King David's Jerusalem for Walt Whitman's Manhattan and Emily Dickinson's Amherst. My opposition was to myself.

All that time I lived apart, as if in seclusion, like I was a hermit on a dirt road in the backcountry. I didn't stay in touch. I didn't reach out. I didn't keep up. I wrote poems. I taught. I walked the dogs. I drank. And, for anyone who asked, I characterized myself as retired from Judaism to indicate, not hostility, but an evacuation, removal, withdrawal, a fall back, an ebb.

I had to wonder, though, as I walked along the bayou, was coming home for a day motivated by something else?

Reconciliation? A hunger for the nod and salute of affirmation? Or, because of the terrible floods, would I see the place, in its metamorphosis, as desirable? Was I now just a threadbare literary man of gratitude for the past? Had my rebellion mellowed? Had I finally reached the end of my one-time future?

I looked across the brown waters of the bayou—my old haunt, where I walked each morning to school, where I used to run away and linger and brood about mystery and destiny, where, without any trouble, I could name many of the families that once lived in these houses, and where once I wished to become no one.

Such a benign, mercurial vision though also a reassurance, something like a promise of the subconscious, an unfolding, like a fantasy, something that had long been remote and mysterious to me, happened next. It was a memory of laughter, walking with Shelly Rose outside her house on Lymbar Drive. She's sixteen years old. In the darkness, she bends over, and then straightens to snap her long hair behind her head. It falls in layers around her eyes and cheeks. Her face is flushed, feathery. She's like a pale bird that's just flown down from the clouds. She moves in the tense air to the intimate rhythm required by an impossible memory, and, all at once, I understood that whatever I once did here, for better or for worse, was still bound up with her story.

I detoured toward Hillcroft and plunged into the backstreets, when the wind slammed a screen door shut—I was about to walk over to my old house on Loch Lomond when the thought of walking past Shelly's house captivated me.

So far, my walking tour had become an act of imaginary excavation. As far as they occurred, what insights I had came not from making a figuration of a time or tunneling into a phantasmal archive in my head, but from studying the menagerie of streets and destroyed homes.

When I finally run out of homes, will that finally be home—
not a landscape or structure, but a condition?

How often have I stood beneath the sturdy roof of my
house in Portland, with the misty rain like a shiver outside the
windows, thinking of this place where the bayou's peppery
water runs low, where my notion of space and distance and
dimension was first determined?

Walking slowly, I felt closer to whole than I had felt in a
long time, as if I was waking from sleep and newly primitive.
Perhaps, by the very act of leaving Texas, and never coming
back, the contest between loss and antagonism became my best
memory, the permanent baseline of what I think of as home.

W hen I reached the center of Lymbar Drive, I stood directly
outside Shelly Rose's small white house. Because we had dated
during junior and senior high school, everything about where I
was standing was intensely familiar. Easy to imagine her bright
kitchen with blinding sun from the west in the late afternoon.
Easy to imagine her bedroom under the front window, the
warm bedspread, a soap opera on television after school. Got
to watch my stories, she'd say, while her older sister, Janise,
answered a ringing telephone in the kitchen. Easy to picture
the slender hallway to her parents' bedroom. The dimly lit living room.

Everywhere on Lymbar there was evidence of families and
children. The aroma of a barbecue grill in the warm wind like
a mood floating weakly from one gradation to another. There
were voices from a few houses down. Those people were
strangers to me now. Like a cloud slowly gathering from a distance, a flimsy happiness took over. It was as if I knew where
I was, and also like I couldn't remember where I was. The
uncertainty was heady.

Do you visit often? I imagined asking an imaginary Shelly in
her fifties now, like me, on the sidewalk under the leafy trees. She

had left the city decades ago, I'd heard. No, she says, I've lost my connection except that friends keep me coming back. You know them all. You? I pictured a wide mouth, and felt something like joy, then sorrow. I pictured her dressed in a blouse with a stitched neckline, collarbone sharp, and her light skin thin with age. Pictured her making an effort of cheerfulness. My last visit was for a funeral, she says. It was a brief visit, is all. I'm so busy anyway, one of us says. Hmm-mmm, she says. What's it like to come back? I say. What do you want to know? she says. Did you get what you wanted from leaving here? I say. I didn't want to leave. I wanted to stay. You know that. Did you? Did I what? I say. Get what you want? By leaving? she says and with her right hand rubs two fingers against her collarbone.

The sky behind her is the color of blue shells.

The walk felt like a failure. I had arrived in Houston like an actor playing myself who is possessed with questions. Who am I, or who do I believe I am? Who was I when I lived here as a boy? Are we the same or different? Can we be reunited?

The same held when I thought of the woman who is Shelly Rose. Were we both hiding a life, like leaving a penny on the street to be found later? But now that I've come back to look for it, it's gone.

The morning before I flew to Texas I woke up from the sound of shouting outside an open window. It must have been a neighbor in the apartment building next door. The sound erupted inside me, stark as a bat. I found my way into the bathroom, and looked in the mirror. In the dark, my eyes were a pastel smear. I looked down the trail of my face, nose, mouth, and chin. The features came through slowly, like dozens of layers of thin glaze smeared on the glass with my fingers. A slight blurring around my forehead. Shadows outside the mouth. A barely perceptible gradation of tones from light to dark. My hair a grainy brown.

I don't know what is about the stranger in the mirror that so appalls. Or is it appeals? I suppose it's the bristling corroboration that the past, which we value, is pervasive, staring back. Is that my life, I think, watching myself, in horror, in a daze? I think to say to the figure in the mirror, Look, Bub, to you I'm a secularist, but to God I'm the loyal opposition.

Wendy was stirring in bed, patting the two dogs that had climbed in and lay across her legs while checking news alerts on her phone that pinged overnight. Since the time we met she has been talking about the thrill of keeping one's inner life intact, to preserve one's umbra of intensity and to tend to what we hold dear.

For her, that's one of the emotional labors of home.

Twelve years ago, one of the first afternoons we spent together, in the springtime, we arranged to meet at the Byways Café in the Pearl district in downtown Portland. We sat outdoors. There was a derelict lot across the street covered with rocks and weeds and pieces of scrap iron, and in the distance was the Willamette River. Together we explored the collision of streets of our pasts, and we prowled through the names of neighborhoods we had apartments in when we both lived in Washington, DC, in the 1990s, but didn't know each other yet, when we were both in our twenties, in graduate school, in love with other people.

It was an unusually warm, sun-filled spring that year in Portland, and we were nothing but two people who felt the demands adult life made upon us. For a few hours we allowed ourselves to be lifted into the iron of confusion that was everywhere, the two of us bobbing like dots in a dangerous, unsparing world, where whatever losses we brought with us that afternoon rested in the corners of the busy café, rested below the tables and chairs, along the windowsills. Like me, she didn't seem wary but found magnetic the pains and sorrows of life, such that a feeling of trust, a sweet languor, spread over us, through our arms and legs and fingers and eyes and mouths, as if that would be our resolution to the enigma. I asked if she thought she would want to live in this city her entire life.

—My parents live in Oregon. In the town they grew up in. The town I grew up in. I talk to my mother every morning on the telephone. I can't see leaving. You?

—Live in Portland?

—Go back to Texas?

—I doubt they'd have me, I said, without explaining, and, to change the subject, asked about her experience as a Catholic.

—I like the aromas, the unnatural rituals, the incense, the Latin, the strange solitude.

—Is that what you're seeking?

—The quiet. The contemplation. It's my way to defend the spirit.

—Yours? Against what?

—All the commotion. Is that how it is for you?

—There's nothing but commotion in a synagogue. Not that it matters. I'm retired from Judaism, I said.

When we had finished drinking our coffees, Wendy took out knitting. I took a compact notebook out of my blazer pocket and put it on the table between us. She was wearing a small denim jacket. She did not take it off the whole time we sat there across the table from each other. Her cheeks were glowing from the easy warmth in the spring air. Her body was lean and angular. She picked up her needles and traced the shapes with them. Her fingers, playing with the black yarn, gave me a feeling of peace. I was wearing jeans and boots, and I said something about dressing the same way for thirty years ever since I was fourteen, that she might find my attire dull.

Finally I heard Wendy sit up out of bed and walk downstairs to make coffee, relieved that she was awake, even as I was absolutely alone in the bathroom, looking at myself in the mirror like some wild man shrieking in the far wilderness.

It's inexplicable to me, in moments like that in the bathroom, that bear no real weight, moments that sprawl and open and quickly close, how so many multitudes can coexist.

As morning came on, and I started to walk the dogs in Laurelhurst Park, I had a strange thought the way we all do, a strange thought out of nowhere, an image of something from the past that skids inside your brain—the face of a lost friend, a city street at midnight, that black scarf you haven't seen in months.

Walking the dogs near the narrow pond under a thicket of intensely silent, tall firs, all the black branches drawn out, twisting, interlocked, under a light drizzle, I saw in my mind teenage boys in a living room, guys perched on the arm of a sofa right next to me, my legs crossed at the ankles. Blue jeans. Cowboy boots. A soft Texas light in the windows. There was Greg Lerner, Randy Reichstein, and Gregg Esses squeezed together, as if we were posing inside a snapshot. All of us fourteen years old. 1978. It was an Esquires house party. Esquires was the Jewish junior high fraternity in Meyerland. Frank Karkowsky and Danny Markoff and Michael Friedman talking behind us about whether they would fight for America or Israel if the two countries went to war. I would go into the Israeli army, says Markoff, arms crossed with a determined look through thick eyeglasses. Karkowsky shrugs, sets down his paper cup of soda pop and tugs on the edges of his flannel shirt. He finds pen and paper and draws a large map of the United States about the size of a football. Next to that he draws a tiny map of Israel shaped like a bent paper clip. No contest, he says and slams the pen on the formica counter. To fight against the Jews, it's against our faith, says Friedman, pulling a white ivy cap over his eyes.

The debate has been forgotten several days later by the time Danny Markoff breaks a tackle and runs four yards across the lawn outside Kerry Rudy's house on Braesvalley Road. A huddle of guys plots the next play, then lines up for the scrimmage. Ricky Reed on one end. Maury Magids next to him in blue baseball sleeves. All of us listening to the cadence. The weather is roasting hot. Friedman sets to take the snap, eyes scanning the grassy yard. He steps back and passes to Markoff,

who's chased out of bounds between parked cars. Later, we're
gathered at Shelley Chaskin's house. A blue swimming pool.
Cannonball splashes from Karkowsky and Lerner. The water
splatting over the hot pavement. They come up singing in uni-
son to the track on the turntable: If you want my body, and you
think I'm sexy, come on, Sugar, let me know. Grass is thick, and
the fencing brown. Bikinis. Short shorts. Shouting and pinch-
ing. Now Reichstein is hauling someone's bicycle onto the roof
of the garage. Indoors, Valerie sits on the kitchen counter, talking into a yellow telephone mounted to the wall, one hand over
her ear so she can hear when her mother insists she come home.
Marcy Dubinsky is at the sink rinsing glasses. She's wearing a
red button-down, and flared pants. Ellen Gilbert stands nearby
leaning against the door, watching the phone call. Her fingers
shoved into her jeans pockets. She watches Hauser in the living
room put on a new album, and Robert Fisher is shouting to
put it on track eleven. The needle groves through the static:
Is this the real life? Is this just fantasy? God save the Queen!
Ellen shouts, then covers her mouth to stifle a laugh. Valerie
can't hear into the phone. Down the hall is an overflow of
shouts, followed by laughter wafting over that. Some rumor
that somebody has a crush on somebody. Followed by a denial.
In the living room there are whoops and hollering. Lauren
Reiter has wrapped her arm around Gail's neck and covered
Gail's mouth with her own hand. She's pulling Gail's head tight
to her face and kissing the back of her own hand, and Gail is
reaching around Lauren's shoulders to hug her affectionately.
I didn't know she could make out like that, shouts Gail once
they pull away. Lauren stands to bow, blows kisses with her
hands. Later, in a pack, we all walk on the footpath above the
bayou to the Jewish Community Center as the late sun filters
through thin clouds. Crickets everywhere. Hauser is running
down the bank. You can't hear what he's shouting. You just
see him skipping near the water and racing back up the slope,
with his long hair floppy and sweaty over his ears. Lauren
and Gail and Ellen circle on their bicycles. Mike Kaplan has

stopped, hands on hips, to say words to Linda Joachim. Mindy Steinberg and Mimi Goldstein move closer to listen. The humid wind has died down. Our mouths move. We are lifted like scarves. Bright and gaudy atop the sharp grass.

Most all of us in Esquires attended Johnston Junior High School, which sits low to the ground on Wigton Drive across from the footbridge over a shallow stretch of the Chimney Rock Road ditch. Each morning before school, from seventh to ninth grades, I locked my bicycle to a post under the awnings and gathered with friends at a spot on the breezeway nicknamed Jew Corner. A lot of the kids from the synagogue's grade school found the transition to public school hard. Halls and classrooms were a universe of rules. When boys got into trouble with one algebra teacher, he summoned us to his desk to insist we turn around so our backsides faced the students, then whacked us several times with a fraternity paddle.

Johnston was in the business of indoctrinating students to accept systems of conformity. No talking, no tardiness, no untucked shirts, no untied shoelaces, no body-revealing clothing, no chewing gum, no smoking, no running. So many of the teachers were unimaginative and unthinking, almost childish, their authority became an obstacle. Every day a different boss every fifty minutes. Those years were my first time making friends with lots of non-Jewish kids. Baptists and Catholics, evangelicals, Hispanic, Vietnamese, Chinese, and African American friends. Each morning seventeen school buses with African-American and Hispanic kids bused from other wards in the city arrived in Meyerland at the junior high and departed at three o'clock in the afternoon in a single convoy. From 1876, when Texas ratified a new state constitution, until the 1970s, racially segregated public schools had been coded into Texas law. In response to the busing movement, a counter-desegregation magnet school system emerged, so that whites could switch schools to avoid minorities. It did seem clear at Johnston that we were all living by different rules, the Jewish and white kids and the African American and Hispanic kids. We were bound by different historical chains as much as by different school zones. There wasn't any nuance to it either. And yet, together, we all pursued the usual dumbed down worksheets and rote drills so that we could be tested for our ability to spit the data back. All of us straggling like cattle to the ringing of bells and avoiding people bigger than you, minding your own business, not asking a question of an adult you knew the adult couldn't answer. I could tell immediately that anyone who asked too many probing questions was considered disrespectful. Worse, you were believed to be threatening, rebellious, too interested in sex, a pot head.

T here were lots of reasons to join Esquires.

My friends joined, not so much out of high seriousness, but as an expression of belonging. Joining Esquires in Meyerland between seventh and ninth grades, was meant to initiate a lasting connection to the Jewish people, to find meaning in Judaism beyond the synagogue, and to develop Jewish identity in Texas. There was absolute commitment to the State of Israel in it and dedication to social service. I joined Esquires with something of a secret ambition. Even while I was just hanging out with the guys, in the folds of my imagination I already knew, from the first day, I wanted to become president of the club, just as my oldest brother Scott had been years before. Like we were the Meyerland Kennedys.

There was no equivalent sorority in Meyerland for junior high girls, so the girls our age were included in all the Esquires' activities. Every six months a new set of officers took over to lead the club, as well as a new sweetheart, one girl from the neighborhood, in eighth or ninth grade, whom the boys voted in, and whose family offered their home as a gathering place for all these Jewish junior high kids to come by, afternoons after school and weekends, on their bicycles.

One January afternoon, when I was in ninth grade and

president of Esquires, I accompanied the rabbi and a few kids from the older Jewish youth organizations to the Seven Acres Jewish Home for the Aged on Chimney Rock Road for an unusual meeting. I'd ridden my bike alongside the bayou against a sharp wind, and arrived first. Waiting outside, I stomped my boots and hugged my arms together in the cold sunshine among a stand of lean pine trees in front of the brick complex. We'd made class trips to the Home when I attended school at Beth Yeshurun, shuffling door to door in the gloomy halls to say hello to the residents. The air in the building smelled of milk. Silver mezuzahs on every doorframe untouched by sunlight.

A few months before, the Esquires had used Mitzvah Day as a work crew to clean up the grounds of the facility, touching up paint, collecting garbage, raking flower beds, sweeping walkways. Most of the high school Jewish youth groups, the local chapters of the national B'Nai Brith Youth Organizations, did something similar every year, more than once. Now, as president of Esquires, I'd learned along with other youth leaders that residents were complaining. So many kids coming around was a nuisance. A group of residents was in revolt.

We gathered at a table in the dining hall, about six of us kids with Rabbi Segal, and the representative of the residents, Mr. Silverman, who was dressed in a blue blazer. Mr. Silverman had a long face and thick hands, gray hair frayed across his forehead from one ear to the other, and two gold chains. Hovering around us all was Mr. Silverman's pungent cologne, along with the smell of disinfectant mixed in with an aroma of cooked corn and baked bread. The other kids sat close together, a polished crowd of argyle sweaters, pastel polos, pullovers, docksiders, and bangles. With his gold rings shining, Mr. Silverman tapped his fingers on the table, curling one of his hands into the shape of a fist as the rabbi spoke about how much trust he had in us, the youth groups, to remember their elders. The rabbi pointed around the table and explained he'd known some of us for may years, most of our lives.

—These aren't wild kids, Mr. Silverman. Other night I was out jogging and a car drove by. Something like five or six kids piled in there. The car slowed, the windows were open. And these rotten kids are shouting expletives at me. Then one of them throws a water-soaked towel that struck me in the leg. That's not these kids. They're trying to do the right thing even when no one is looking.

—They should find somewhere else to do their thing. Enough's been done here. Check off your Mitzvah Day box someplace else, kids. Hear what I'm saying? said Mr. Silverman.

—We have to do Mitzvah Day. It's required, the president of the BBYO group known as Loeb said.

He was a lean high school junior with blow-dried hair parted down the middle. He looked at his friend from SAR, also a high school junior, who began talking immediately.

—I believe that people make long journeys in life, Mr. Silverman, and that here, at the Home for the Aged, they can find a form of higher meaning. We help provide that.

Mr. Silverman's expression was flat, and the rabbi cleared his throat.

—It's important for us to help them, Mr. Silverman. We must teach our children diligently, as it says in Deuteronomy. You can understand that, sir. Can't you?

—Why are you here, rabbi?

—I have congregants in this facility, as you know. I would never turn away any person who asked me to perform a Jewish function, whether they're a member of my shul or not. I feel these youngsters should learn the same. Ok by you? the rabbi said, and his cheeks slackened.

Mr. Silverman looked down at his rings, then he looked at me, the youngest at the dining table.

—What can he do for me?

One of the high school girls spoke up.

—If I may, Mr. Silverman, our group, Malev, has been coming to Seven Acres for many years, doing a makeup day with the ladies. Last year we came for a day and delivered Hanukah cards. We'd hate to lose that.

—Ok, honey. And this one? No offense, son. What are you? Twelve? With the cowboy boots? And the snap buttons? Going to a rodeo? Mr. Silverman said, pointing at me with a fat thumb, then fingering his gold chains.

—Fifteen next month, I said.

—Come on, rabbi. Fourteen?

These were the years especially when I thought of becoming a rabbi.

At that moment I could feel both the bizarre mood at the table and an ominous mood in my head converge. The weekend before was the Esquires Temple Night in the main sanctuary at Beth Yeshurun. The guys served as ushers and led prayers, and I gave a brief sermon. Looking down at the swooping rows of plush seats of the sanctuary without any anticipation of falling, I delivered a sermon on charity. I had given special attention to the way the congregants' eyes followed my words. But one man stood during the middle of the sermon and gathered his things to leave. I wanted to stop speaking right then and let everyone watch him walk up the long sloping aisle. Where did he think he was going? Did he think he could just walk out as I spoke about duty and generosity? Did he think he could walk out on all these sons and daughters of Judea inside Meyerland? What could this odd-looking deserter—removing his yarmulke even before he reached the impossibly quiet doors to walk into the bright foyer—be thinking, his back to the Holy Ark? I might have shouted, Sir, is there something out there we don't know about? I told Shelly about what went through my head afterward, and she said, You just don't like people, that's all. I like people, I said.

I looked at Mr. Silverman. I spoke slowly, leaning on a genteel drawl.

—I don't know, Mr. Silverman. We're just kids. You got me there. We're kids. I'm the youngest. Esquires is mostly thirteen and fourteen year-olds. These guys around the table are all in high school. They drove their cars here. I rode my bike. But, I think we have something to offer. Even us. Even Esquires. OK? Even the fourteen year olds. I know it's a lot, all these groups, to come up here all the time. We can cut back. Esquires will cut back. How's that? We want to give our time, if you'll have it. Even if it's just once every couple years, is all. We have our enthusiasm and our time. That's it. We're just kids. We have a desire to do something. I don't have family here at Seven Acres personally. But because I went to the Day School at Beth Yeshurun, I've come to Seven Acres many times over the years. OK? We've met, you and I. First time I was here on one of those visits I think I was in kindergarten. We sang Passover songs. You may not like us here all the time, but others don't feel that way.

He pushed his tongue into his cheek.

—We really just want to do the smallest things. We're good at washing cars. Need your car washed? My guys love to play poker. Last month we had Stag Night. Blackjack. Dice. How about that?

Everyone laughed, except Mr. Silverman, who was pushing his lips out, and nodding. I peeked at the rabbi and back at Mr. Silverman.

—Care to make it interesting? I said.

—He understands the mitzvah of *gemilut hesed,* Mr. Silverman. Can't deny that, said the rabbi using the Hebrew for the concept of bestowing a kindness.

—Here's the deal. Take it or leave it. Three events a year, and you all work it out.

—There are six groups here. How about one a year for each of us, I said and Mr. Silverman agreed, saying, You should go into politics, kid, and he reached across the table to shake my hand, gripping it firmly.

Outside the Home, after the others had driven off in their cars, the rabbi stood with me near my bicycle in the cold air under a billowing sky. He was dressed in an overcoat and gloves, white smoke coming out of his breath. That man, the rabbi was saying, he should thank God every day for his eye-sight, for his good teeth, for his ability to breathe, to use the bathroom. You know, there's a prayer for pissing and poop-ing? What hair-splitting—why are you here? Oy. Men with clenched fists can't shake hands, young man. Well you won the day. Mazel tov.

I was elated. Everything seemed written. Beyond serenity I felt the life created for me was my life.

It occurred to me, as I walked along the bayou toward my old house, that I might, in the end, understand very, very little about what I was looking for.

This prompted a new round of questions. Where do I wish to be going with these thoughts while I'm walking around here? Or, where am I going with these thoughts?

A warm wind bleached the houses. Everything appeared precious, poignant: the sun-dried grass, flies and mosquitoes in the dense light, a truck beeping while backing up. Beside each house there might be roses along a fencepost, a scraggly hedge, a walkway of patterned stones, a watering can sitting on a porch step, the sun coughing toward the horizon, kids on bicycles pedaling in ragged huffs, a Texas flag hoisted to the side of one house, with the white star fluttering.

Looking around, I wanted to think the past was safe.

But looking at the empty lots and the boarded up houses damaged from the flooding, I realized that we know the past, not because it survived, but because we have. With slight reinterpretations, even misconceptions, we fabricate what we think of as the past. We color old beliefs and fears and hopes. The raw materials remain the same, but our memories give it a shape that makes it into something different, like a con-jecture. What we understand memory to be—a sequence of images, a moment in time, an era, a kaleidoscopic feeling kept from oblivion—is a sensory experience more than a factual one. The past is always changing into something else because we make it change. I mean, can I even accept what it is I'm allegedly remembering? Isn't my current self simply refiguring my former self, whoever that was, as a new disfigurement? Was I really so savvy with Mr. Silverman?

Cars rolled by appearing to go nowhere. A small boy in football pads pedaled past me on his bike. Near a stop sign, I heard bits of talk radio from passing cars. From an old-time country station came chords from Linda Ronstadt's "Silver Threads and Golden Needles" with its rollicking backbeat, the lyrics like a swig of ice-cold water. I took note of the fading blue and red colors of an old Houston Oilers bumper sticker on one of the cars, and I remembered the Monday night Oilers football game Shelly and I went to in the fall of 1978, against the Miami Dolphins, and the closing minutes when the home team needed a big play, and Shelly says, Do you believe in prayer? And I said, I believe in Earl Campbell.

The whole feeling in the Astrodome was suspense and dread that night. Fifty thousand stomping and shaking and shouting. There was a bumping of knees and elbows and hips. Babble and hubbub. Reckless cries. Mangle of faces. A high wave of human sound week twelve of a miracle season. We believed we were freeing ourselves from bondage, after years of dispirited football in Houston, a shattered glare in our eyes from all the losing. There was still the old expectation that the extraordinary will happen on the other side, but on our side the pratfall, the choke, the grail that must remain untouched. Beer venders were shuffling up the steps, glancing over their shoulders at the start of every play. Sweet beer! Cold beer! Coldest foam in the Dome! Come on now! Cold beer! Sweet beer! Three! Here! Right here, brother! That's it. Pass it down. Don't spill. Watch it. Careful now. Atta boy. Quick spills. Foam-flick. Peanut shells underneath our feet. Aroma of cotton candy. Everywhere blue-and-white pompoms swishing like powder.

It was a night for Shelly and me that made us feel we might

never again be tired. Something happened during the game. A purity had found us. A triumph had wrinkled into our blood. We wanted to resist nothing. It was as if we were birds hurrying in the air along with the breeze, clear, and concise, and tinged with blue.

Ever since Sid Gillman was hired as head coach in 1973, the Oilers and Meyerland had a special bond. Gillman's Jewishness was storied, and he made a point of having players come to shul to promote the team. Some of my friends took great pleasure in the rumor Gillman avoided studying Torah as a boy and instead focused on sports. He was nearly hired head coach at Ohio State University but was passed over. Similarly at Illinois, Purdue, and Minnesota. I was an ambitious sucker, Gillman said, every time a job would open up, I would try. But as soon as they found I was a Jew, that was the end of it. In 1955 the Los Angeles Rams pursued Gillman to become their head coach. Before he accepted he said to Dan Reeves, the general manager, I have to tell you something: I'm Jewish. To which Reeves said, Maybe that will help.

Now the Oilers were coached by Bum Phillips, who made his way through the city with the charm of a horseshoe nailed to the side of a barn. Bum spoke in a Texas vernacular we all knew as homespun. Told that one of his running backs was struggling with a drill where he was supposed to run backwards, Bum told his assistant coach, Damn if I care if he can run backwards, we're only gonna run him forwards. That autumn Monday night in 1978, Bum was attired in flared blue jeans, a paisley patterned snap-buttoned shirt with a large, flat, open collar, sleeves buttoned at the wrist, and green alligator-skin cowboy boots that, from time to time, he kicked at the painted hashmarks. On his nose were gigantic peach-colored glasses.

They got to get mad, they got to get ferocious, Shelly kept saying when the game seemed to go the Dolphins' way. Our guys are like scholars, she says at the very moment quarterback Dan Pastorini, number seven, heads to the line of scrimmage deep in our own territory at the nineteen yard line, second and seven, and Earl Campbell lines up behind him, his blue jersey, number 34, barely tucked into his white britches. Earl Campbell had legs that were like tree trunks with cleats. Lot of guys tried to tackle him low, but if you hit him in the thighs you were likely to bounce off. He said he was embarrassed if he got tackled by just one man. Earlier in the season, Earl— everyone just called him Earl—cleared the line of scrimmage only to find a beefy linebacker there to met him. With his head and shoulders the defender hit Earl right in the thighs. The players paused, sure Earl was stopped. But it just delayed him, is all. Earl brushed the linebacker aside as easily you might gently toss a small child during a pillow fight. Five yards later it took four guys to carry him down—one wrapped his arms around Earl's waist, two more converged in front to stop his forward momentum, while another grabbed him from the back. He could outrun you too—he slipped through tackles like he was stepping in and out of a hula hoop. Now Houston was only up by five. Minutes on the clock. The crowd like one ecstatic cry at the snap when Pastorini pitches wide to Earl who gathers the ball into his right hand like he's holding a loaf of bread. He breaks a tackle in the backfield, moves past an- other Dolphins player and turns up field alongside the sideline in front of the Oilers's bench. Now he's moving past defenders who appear to be standing still, opening up, staying ahead of everyone. The 50, the 45, 40, the 35. Earl is blazing along the white chalk of the sidelines. He's taking over the game. The defenders are falling a long way back. All the Dolphins are dropping back. Earl is running like a machine. He's all alone. He is going to score an 81 yard touchdown.

The crowd goes berserk. Pompoms shake like powder-blue snow. On the scoreboard there's the head of a yellow steer. Texas flag blasting out of one horn. American flag blasting out of the other. Smoke snorted from the steer's nostrils in bright red clouds. Fifty thousand fans sing the Oilers fight song and there's a surge through the Astrodome a surge through the city's bars and restaurants, a surge through the living rooms. From Kingwood to Clear Lake, North Shore to South Shore, Sugar Land to Meyerland, all of us stomping and shaking and shouting as one city.

A House Toward Evening

As the afternoon light flattened, I stood at the corner of my old street and took in the fragrant silence.

Stepping on the sidewalk was a feeling of entering something completely open like a balcony. Sunlight sending patches onto the grass from house to house, the rays descending through the branches in a fan of spires. The single-storied, brick, mid-century moderns stared at each other with adoration, like long-married couples, under a leafy canopy that held from curb to curb. Each house faced an unwrinkled lawn, driveways ironed flat. Unlike so many other streets, except for the addition of a gabled roof, new garage, fresh plantings, Loch Lomond appeared unchanged from the floods.

Here, a car door slammed. The beep-beeping of a lock.

Above the houses large clouds, patterned by the sunlight, separated like floating milkweed spores.

To get to Loch Lomond I had crossed Endicott Lane and took notice of the new constructions that were replacing the torn-out houses. Mossy trees had been stripped out of the ground as troublesome as weeds. Signage outside a teardown read, CUSTOM CLASSICS. Empty lots were like the remnants of archeological sites. So many houses were sledgehammered and pickaxed to make way for the new. Work proceeded on a home construction and the jagged walls jutted upward. Then on comes the roof until finally you can no longer remember even the empty lot when only the naked foundation had remained, and along with it the former dramas of the people who used to live there—old crossbeams chucked into a rusting dumpster the most moving illustration of how temporary our dwellings are. Gone the various sizes of beds and chests of drawers, patches of blue sky peered at through odd shapes of windows, the old protections from sun and rain, papered walls, locks that once had stubbornly maintained shelter along with the tastes and habits of the people who lived there—what had been distinctive and what each family offered to the human story of eating and sleeping and making love and pitching a fit, the magnanimity of doing things in close proximity to one another. In the end, we are all pitilessly exposed. Soon faces would peer out of new windows and doors, or disappear in the unknowable twists of a family's desires.

This felt like the meaning of absence to me, perhaps even the meaning of memory. Not missing something, but being on the outside. As I had felt on Lymbar outside Shelly Rose's house, as I was feeling now on Loch Lomond, I felt a wish to be invisible, as if I could embody perspective only, like a line of vision. I understood I had been having something like a romantic affair all these years with my long absence from Texas, a sense in which the life I have lived might be the one that's completely fictitious. Had I made up the whole thing? This former life? Because I couldn't imagine how my two lives might be stitched together. In that moment I felt I was no one in either place, and that all the walking had led to this new reprimand.

The intensity, however, owed everything to feeling calmly oriented, like I could see through time, unterrified of abandonment, wild as a torn heart, and with no care for what I was waiting to see, to possess nothing even, and finally to accept what secrets of life were about to be revealed.

Behind me there was the scraping teeth of a push broom against the concrete, and a white man with a tidy beard was walking quickly. I stepped over a set of drapes set out for free on the curb and nodded to an Asian woman dressed in flowing blue slacks, who walked by without looking back. A car revved down the block.

My old house rose fully intact like a strange island. I looked at the brick facade, black shutters, and triangular roof as if looking in from sea, with the thick green grass washed up to the shaded patio. I thought to peer through the windows to see if all the secrets the house held were still there—the hallway down from the kitchen with its blue flowery wallpaper and faint dust, and nothing happening. But I stayed still. Each step of the walk had stacked up to where I was standing alone on the empty sidewalk, absorbed in the passage, where the myths of a life, when you least expect them, appear, fall away, and reassert themselves.

Two boys came pedaling by no-handed on their bikes on their way home from school, taunting each other and throwing a football at the same time. They biked alongside one another close enough to trade punches in the shoulder.

I felt a need for something, pure as a word.

O nce, a few years before that day, I was about to fly to Houston to give a lecture and was surprised to find myself in an email correspondence with Gail Gerber. We'd not been in touch for decades. A financial advisor, Gail has been living in and about Meyerland with her husband and family all these years. She wrote to say she'd seen a notice about the event and hoped to attend. This was followed for several days by a buoyant email exchange, back and forth, this and that, about where and what and how things are going. Linda wants to come, too, Gail wrote. I knew she meant Linda Joachim.

Word is getting around, Gail emailed next. How would you feel about a small reunion?

How would I feel? It was a long time, wasn't it, since I was the seventeen-year-old kid who stalked out of the synagogue on a bright spring day for the last time, kicked out by the rabbi, with all of my friends watching with alarm, and with the whole of my life ahead of me to discover what is out here? That kid with a bundle of objections under his arm that Judaism adulterates the origins of the cosmos, that it manages to combine prayer with solipsism, that its system of indoctrination is grounded on magical, wishful thinking?

And yet, weren't all my objections what I took to be the truest meaning of home, what I was against?

Over email, we bandied names for the reunion: Michael, Valerie, Tracy, Debbie, Randy, Greg, Mindy, Lauren, Robert, Jimmy, Neil, Frank, Marcy, Ellen, Patti, Shelly, Karen, Jeff, Heather, Greg, and others. First names only. No need for last names for a gathering of litter mates.

After the lecture, Gail threaded her way to the front of the auditorium and we embraced. I'd have recognized her anywhere, with her energetic talk, quizzical eyes, easily amused as ever. About an hour later I was met at the door of her two-story house by three women. Linda Joachim, who had attended the reading. Marcy Dubinsky, who grew up two blocks from my house and who was the sweetheart of Esquires during my term as president when I was fourteen. And Mindy Steinberg, whose house with a backyard swimming pool we often swam in. Hugs all around. You haven't changed at alls, all around. Them looking at me with blinking eyes like I was a wildcat that just fell out of a tree. Me, blinking back at them. All of us so imprinted to each other I could've picked them out of lineup through a thick fog while wearing a blindfold.

Then as relaxed as you might say, hey or how's it going or good morning to a passerby on the sidewalk, Mindy says, David, where have you been?

So casual, so nonchalant, the way she said it. So effortless, serene, so impromptu. David, where have you been? As if some forty years ago I'd run up to the Stop N'Go behind Braeswood Square to get a case of beer for everyone and never came back.

How do you answer that question to old friends who didn't leave home or, if they had, had long since returned, while you've lived something of a writer's peripatetic life, and you feel certain that people coming to the intimate reunion are now your old neighborhood's accountants, dentists, financial advisors, insurance executives, and lawyers, same as their parents were, same as so many Texas petit bourgeois Jews you defected from, the conformities from which you vanished like the wind. What was going on inside your spirit all this time while you scoured that part of your past, burnished it, purged it, when you wanted to be in discord with yourself and not become like someone seeking roots in a familiar graveyard? What were all those years of being on the lam about, longing to be free of the Jewish streets of Texas, where similarities were uniformly emphasized by parents, almost all of whom were college-educated and had pledged Jewish fraternities and sororities and married in the 1950s or early 1960s, and where stay-at-home mothers volunteered at the synagogue or the temple or the ADL, intent on keeping up appearances, while the fathers drove out of Meyerland each day to be Houston's manufacturers, energy brokers and entertainment executives, bankers and lawyers and shop owners and garbage collectors?

Where had I been?

It's not the years, my dear, I wanted to say to Mindy. It's the mileage.

More so, there's the side B of that question, which I've been fingering in my pocket, ever since that reunion, like a broken shard of a tombstone.

Why did you never come back? Why did you never come back to this place you've all but memorized, at least memorialized in so much of your writing, in order to make yourself, at the very least, visible to yourself?

I felt a vibrating space between old friends and me inside Gail's beautiful house, so welcoming, all of them. I was thinking about what some of them had to say about the time when we were kids sharing these streets, and their stories were like a door creaking open. Debbie Boniuk talking about the report cards we got from Beth Yeshurun, with grades for Hebrew penmanship. Marcy Dubinsky talking about what she called the snotty side of Meyerland south of the bayou. Mindy Steinberg laughing over how she and Lauren Reiter rode their ten-speed bikes, dressed in nothing but a bikini top and terry cloth shorts, past Hillcroft all the way to Sharpstown Mall to buy high-heeled shoes for an Esquires Temple Night and dance. Frank Karkowsky describing how all the fathers drove their fourteen-year-old kids across Meyerland to pick up their fourteen-year-old dates for that Temple Night—plus two other couples—to drop them all off at shul where we served as ushers and led the service, and another father picks the six of us up and drives us to the Fondren Club for a jukebox dance party, and how, at night's end, a third father drives everyone home across this sleepy corner of the city. Karkowsky says, My dad parked outside my date's house. That was you, Gail, remember? I do, she says. I was wearing a tan dress, tied at the waist. I still have the pictures, she says. Karkowsky says, we were parked in the circle drive of your parents's house on South Braeswood, and you had already stepped out of the car and said good bye and thank you and all that, and I was just sitting in the front seat with the window rolled down—unbuttoning my suit vest, loosening my tie—when I felt an elbow shot hard into my ribs, and my dad says, Walk her to the door, son. Here Michael Friedman says, we were so isolated in Meyerland when we grew up. From grade school all the way until high school, he says, I thought Houston was something like eighty percent Jewish. Lot of good that did, Valerie Roosth says, our little Jewish Meyerland was such a closed world. Either you were in or out. Then she moans, literally moans.

They talked too about what it was like to raise their own children here. And yet, throughout the night, as I talked with this person or that one, each of them, in some variation or another, and without a layer of indifference, leaned toward me, in a whisper, to say, in response to something, Well, David, you left.

I didn't ask, what do you mean by that? I knew I was being accused of seeking meaning elsewhere, of trying to nullify what had once brought us together, that, by my absence, I was suggesting life in Meyerland was meaningless. But it stung. I had always thought my restlessness was a gift. Restless was when I felt most content.

Now, standing on the sidewalk on Loch Lomond, across the street from my house, I kicked at the grass, like a horse pawing the ground.

Looking toward the front windows, I imagined my father and me taking in a college football game on television on a Saturday afternoon. I'm five years old. See how they line up now, he instructs. Watch the quarterback, watch his eyes. I disappear into the quarterback's eyes and see the dark grass on the screen, explosions off the line bursting with dust, the bodies caving and splattering. Quiet now. Watch the quarterback. His eyes. The afternoon flies above us. Wind that can't be heard outside the windows comes and goes in waves so that the trees move. Later, after the game has been turned off, Mother has stepped onto the front porch and stands under the awning to watch my father throw the football to my brothers and me. Thin, young, with quick eyes, she's wearing her black hair short, and glancing at the older boys as they throw the ball between themselves. She can't help imposing her worries about what was between us and the world, even during a game of catch. The very idea of the game, like the world beyond the house, looks dangerous. She keeps her eyes on the ball and on my sweaty brothers, nine and ten years old. Slap of the hands against the brown leather. The ball pulled against the chest. Cheer and groan. Chase after a missed throw. Go deep! One of them sprints to the edge of the lawn and across the next driveway and watches the spiraling ball arc under the sky into his hands. Then my turn, when my father takes a step closer to me as if all that is between us is the length of his arm, and underhand he tosses the ball to me. It spins and spins.

I imagined myself, another time, maybe eight years old, early on a Saturday morning looking through the panes of glass at the lawn and the brick facade of the Hartsfield's house across the street, behind where I was standing. The Brochstein's house next to that. The boy who was me in this memory is leaning against the window, his legs almost trembling, dressed in blue slacks, a suit jacket, white shirt and clip-on tie, dark dress shoes, about to go to shul. A sense of unending time. Gazing time. As if consciousness had not yet begun. A jogger flashes by, bare chested. The newspaper boy pedals a tall bicycle with knobby tires. At my feet Velvet elegantly growls, while the clouds salt the sky. Then a quarrel from another room, followed by surprised faces.

Then it's impossible for me to catch the shape of his cheek. His lips become twisted, his hair thins and begins to gray, his skin wrinkles and fades, peels from his bones until he is a middle-aged man alone on the sidewalk. And what am I to say?

Some days, in southeast Portland, in the fall, late afternoons, when children are across the road on the swing sets at Laurelhurst Park, and the light is soft and low and dropping fast, and the dark waits in the eastern sky to let all its bulk down to within an inch of the ground, I sit on the porch as the leaves twirl like confetti and wonder how did I get here so many thousands of miles from what I feel I know best. Not Douglas fir or red cedar maples or dim rain from November until May, but a nameless, untold, distant, wide-open sky.

The past comes knocking when we least expect it, and we feel like we're the child being called in at dusk—why now, why so soon?—as if called away from the center of everyday existence into some place in the mind where something, you don't know what, has been lost. I like to think I know enough of life not to be hypnotized by the past, that a moment can never wholly be what we think it stands for. And yet, if just fleetingly, we are beneficiaries of its essence.

Being an expatriate Texan, like being a retired Jew, has involved learning how to forget my own consciousness. It can leave me famished, pleading with myself to sponge up new life, to become if not a better person then more unclouded.

What a job it is, because I am still myself.

And yet with all the struggles and breakthroughs nothing can tell you what a pleasure it is to be so alone. It's almost impossible for people who have not experienced it to understand how much delight I can take from preserving some of the nothingness I've felt since leaving Texas, triumphal and grief-struck with a loony, quixotic desire for the white spaces of a different existence, of being released into the world. I've grown comfortable with the losses, as if I am always entering a new, peculiar disposition.

And yet, whenever I think of home, I see it as a distant horizon staggering in and out of view.

It was only ten days after the Esquires banquet at which Shelly Rose became the club's sweetheart, in March, 1979, that I pedaled my bicycle fast up South Braeswood to Hillcroft along the bayou over to her house—with a distant sun in my eyes in the late afternoon.

Valerie had called, crying, saying Shelly's mother had boarded a flight that morning to San Antonio.

—A Beth Israel Sisterhood thing. I know, I said.

—No. No, she flew right back. She was gasping. She came back on the next flight and went to a hospital near the airport, Valerie said, sobs flying out of her throat, and there was a commotion of voices in the background I couldn't make out.

—Gasping?

—She had a heart attack. She had a heart attack right in the examination room. They couldn't revive her. She died. Right in the hospital.

Days earlier, the day after Shelly's fourteenth birthday, she and I had sat on the bed in her bedroom. I'd brought her a small box of candy with flowers as a gift, and I could hear the butcher paper crinkle around the bouquet, which somehow gave the effect of formality to the occasion. Balloons from the banquet flopped across the floor. We were trying to agree to

break up during the six months she was to be Esquire's sweetheart—there was a rule against the girl dating the members—
and all the boys would be coming all summer long to her
house every few days in the afternoons. I'd just completed my
term as the club's president, but I agreed not to come to her
house, not for a few months at least, and one of us proposed
an oath. But there was something else, and neither of us knew
what it was or how to express it. Each time a stretch of silence
gathered, I stared at the trees out the window, and there was
the sound of birds careening from one end of the sky to the
other. Shelly was barefoot, kept kicking the heel of my boots,
saying in a powdery drawl, it's not exactly like breaking up.

It was a dreadful spectacle, an underlying urgency to do
what was required inside the community we were living in. We
sat open mouthed, not trying to camouflage our disappoint-
ment. One moment I was leaning toward her, our eyes almost
touching. In the next we'd pull back, shoulder to shoulder,
unmistakably bewildered, the only witnesses to our lives.

From far up Lymbar cars were already packed bumper to
bumper on both sides of the block. Gathering at the house were
adults in suits and ties or in dress skirts, all standing around
in the front yard in a solemn stillness. Their faces pained,
twisted. Bodies expectant. Everyone walking softly and slow.
Agonized smiles. In their eyes flickered the thousands of other
such gatherings. Every wide-eyed glance, every handshake and
whispered word spoken under a breath, every embrace, every
stifled tear and then letting go of tears, the tossing of a body
back and forth, and then a lethargic stare, lowering of eyes,
invited everyone there to evaluate their lives. The bodies thrust
into the hands and arms of each other with a hum of despair, a
craving for insight.

When I pedaled up to the driveway of the house I saw
Shelly's sister, Janise, standing in the small lawn, head lowered,
surrounded by her high school girlfriends. Her eyes seemed
caved, but filled with an excess of gentleness. She was clasp-
ing her hands together, and two other girls had their arms

around her. Boys and girls from Esquires were milling in the driveway. Valerie was walking vaguely toward me after I stored my bicycle along the side of the brick house. She was dressed in the same clothes she'd been wearing that day at school, her hair pulled back with a hair band, her cheeks red and damp. She won't let anyone at all into her room, Valerie said, she says only you can come in, and at once she insisted I follow her into the house, linking her arm in mine.

There was the sound of plates laid on top of each other coming from the kitchen. Women had been setting out a buffet. Trays of sweets, cold cuts, glasses, and bottles. Overhead lights turned on. Every lamp bright. The people in the house looked taken by surprise. Each room held adults groaning deeply. As if in apology someone was whispering, It's just a mystery. Shelly's father was sitting in a low chair in the living room, dressed in a suit and tie, his face pale. He gave me a sidelong look and nodded when I walked over to him and shook his hand. At first it felt flat and warm inside my palm and then became a loosened circle around my fingers. I heard someone's voice, low: The boyfriend.

Valerie and I pressed through the crowd and found Shelly in her room face down across the bed, shoes off, a long skirt, her blouse untucked, crying into her hands. I closed the door and sat on the bed, the two of us alone. Where have you been? she cried, and heaved her body into the covers.

I had never seen a face so wet from tears. I put a hand on her back and rubbed small circles, like a swirl of mist, up and down her spine, until, after a time, she propped herself onto a pair of pillows, and lifted her head and inhaled hard to catch up the tears back into her eyes. Her hands drifting down from over her lips into her lap, she stared downward and dropped her chin lower. Breathing hard through her mouth and covering her ears with her hands, as if she could hear a scream. She shook her hair, and finally leaned forward with her forehead on my shoulder.

We sat like that a long time, both of us silent. The air in the small room felt dewy inside the aroma of perfume.

Feeling flush, as if in two places at once, I thought of my grandmother's burial in Oklahoma three years earlier. Upright shovels with their blades stuck in a large pile of earth to one side of her grave. Mourners stepping up to throw clumps of dirt onto the coffin. There were so many people at that funeral. I expected it would be the same for Shelly's mother. Mourners would be coming from all over. Women would be weeping, dabbing tears. Men staring rigidly at their dull shoes. At the cemetery, old people would be holding each other, hand in hand, as if suddenly un-practiced in the art of grief. In the humid, windy afternoon, Shelly's grandmother would come close to her at the graveside and put an arm around her, or some other woman, and squeeze her tightly, and the two of them would look at the soil on the lid of the coffin. It's time to go, someone would say, and they would slowly depart, as if unable to empty their minds of what they had just seen. Shovels rasping as men sank the blades into the ground. Wind blowing dirt over the cemetery grass. Dirt they could taste inside their mouths long after they'd folded their bodies into the car and drove home.

How long? she said finally. How long did it take? With your dad? To get back to normal? It's never going to be normal. Is it? Not now, she said and pushed damp strands of hair behind an ear, watching my mouth, as if to imitate my expression. No, I said, then I made a silent response, perhaps something mysterious in my eyes, as if I could pour water into her spirit.

It was three years, almost to the day, a March day, since my father had his stroke, a day I'd come home from school, in the same way that Shelly had, to find life had changed. I found my brothers waiting all alone in Matt's room, both of them crouched on the bed. Don't leave the house, Scott said, your father's going to die. Mother was at the hospital, he said, and I could imagine her squeezing my father's paralyzed left hand while he lay restless on the intensive care cot, and, with her high standards, talking calmly to doctors who were strangers to her, feeling a punch in her stomach when told he could die from complications of the stroke or during tests to find out more. And she's thinking, what to tell the boys? What to tell us to expect? My father didn't die, but the words in his brain would be forever immobilized. Words that once were close to him, spoken when the spirit to speak came upon him, no longer rose inside his mouth, and instead they would flicker off his tongue, like faint whiffs of wind, leaving nothing but a stutter.

Times we'd talk at his place in the Nob Hill Apartments on North Braeswood were occasions for deciphering his idiosyncratic shorthand. After dinner we'd clean up and settle on the blue sofa and talk politics. I'd point to a picture of Ronald Reagan on the cover of *Time* magazine, and I say something like, Reagan's evil. Good woman, he says, mixing up the pronouns. What? It's a him, not her, I say, and he hates government. Yes, he says. You like government, don't you? You get money for disability? Your naval retirement. He taps his chest—home, he says. That's not only yours, I say, the American people pay that, not some faceless, Government-is-the-Problem behemoth. He spreads his arms, but doesn't say anything, thinking about the words, then drops his arms and looks upward. Too fat, he says. Fat? Rubbing two fingers against his thumb, he indicates he means money. Fat, he says. Well we're the wealthiest nation in the history of the world, I say, we can afford to help people. He points to the photograph of Reagan. Good woman, he says. Man, I say. Good....man, he says. Right, I say, but, no, he's not. Woman, he says again. Man, I say. Shah...man...woman, he says, pursing his lips and slowly mouthing the word. He's not a good woman, I say, he's evil. Yours, not mine—you like ABC, he says. This shorthand stumps me again. ABC? Who's ABC? He taps his chest—navy, soup, he says, white soup. I stare at his mouth. White soup? Do you mean clam chowder? Yes. White soup, pretty girl, his husband, he says. ABC? Yes, he says. You mean, JFK? Yes, he says, ABC. No, A...B...K. Soup, he says, pretty girl.

Sitting with Shelly, on her soft bedspread, that March day, I think I wished to outdistance what I knew, to outdistance my own experience, to shed what I previously understood about how life can change, change utterly, without warning, and that words, such as we understood them, are one place where we can find a harbor. I wanted to say something to her about that. But I didn't know how to say anything like that. I knew the sounds but not the words. When Jews mention their dead loved ones, they sometimes say, may their memory be a blessing. The full expression is, may their memory be a blessing in the world to come. The blessing is not conferred upon us but upon the dead, not here, but there. To say something to Shelly about that, to acknowledge this new, uncommon bond that would seal us together for years to come, I just started talking, not sure where I was going with it.

—Imagine walking in the park. It's summertime. You're wandering alone. It's getting dark. The air is shiny. The leaves and grass and bark on the trees are all shiny. Now, picture this. OK? There are birds gathered on the ground, and then they rise up. They're flying into the clouds, wherever they go. They circle right over your head. Then they disappear into the sky into the horizon. They're there, and also they're not there. That's what it's like. There-and-not-there is what's there. Are you with me?

She nodded.

—When you think of them, the birds, after they're gone, that's them being like a blessing. In the sky. In the sky inside you. It never goes away. The change. It's always there, I said.

There was a knock at the door. It was Valerie. You guys? she called from behind the door.

—In a second, Shelly called back.

We held eyes for a moment, the light in the room glowing in spirals. There were more noises at the door.

—Keep talking. I'm in a park. The birds. They're inside me?

—You're thinking of them makes them the blessing. You know? After a while you begin to forget how to look for whatever it is you were looking for and maybe you even forget what it was. You sense other people coming into the park. They're laughing. And you know you just have to stay there for a long time. And press on.

—No choice.

—None.

Soon I stood at the window, while Shelly sat on the bed alone, wiping tears. I felt the AC blow across the hairs on my arms. Outside, between shifting, oversized clouds, ragged patches of fading blue skies sprayed over the trees. There were voices dwindling away toward the living room and kitchen. Agitation mixed in with fuss and tumult. It grew louder as if something happened to someone, then quieted. People stopped at the edge of the hall, crimped with tension, and watched Shelly come out of the bedroom. Some smiled in her direction. So many people cheek to cheek. I lost sight of her after she pushed through the hallway, then found her again in the kitchen bending down toward one of the cabinets to find a long silver tray to give to one of the ladies to put out with more food.

For years afterward, when Shelly and I were together and alone—after her sister had gone to college and she was cooking the meals for her and her father, just as she was handling the chores of the house, dealing with the bills, managing appointments—it sometimes felt like we were always un-wrinkling from that experience on the bed. We became like birds ourselves, whipping higher and lower in a single motion, mounting and dismounting the clouds, seeking the light in a pleasant swoop, but unable, no matter what, to escape ourselves, until finally we just gave up and calmed down, sitting side by side, her head on my shoulder, her loosened strands of hair collecting in my lips.

It's hard to know, from this distance in time, what map was being erased inside our minds right then, what surveys and orientations were being redrawn.

Just as there are days here in Portland with the sheen of

morning light on the Douglas firs and distant figures skirting every so often among the trunks and the low mist splayed over the rooftops, I watch for the softest leaves to glister as if watching for a message. The contemplative thoughts go out and come back with marvelous speed. They bend into themselves, arching, spiraling, warping, into an uninterrupted circle. Or they gather, again and again, as it were, in one spot on the horizon, fixed there, like birds twirling in the dull sky, now to the left, now to the right.

Surely our lives are always rising to the old emptiness, and a great wind keeps carrying us to a place we want, a place we know. Surely the point of returning to the threshold of the past is to find, not the masks we once wore, but the faces underneath.

An autumn of wasps. Mud daubers and yellow jackets. They flew through the grass and under the eaves of houses, lewd and violent, languished on windowsills, or skimmed through opened doorways. From their ground hive, they stirred up, black and yellow, the workers and queen, dappling and buzzing and clicking like broken pieces of wind.

Ever since the day my parents' marriage dissolution was signed in October, Mother had taken to bed. Sitting propped against some pillows without all her usual ferocity, she let the magazines she was reading slip from her hands, and then put her head back and appeared to weep. The deepest well in her heart had dried up. The memory of her marriage she tried to seal away to a perfect absence. Nothing of that life remained. Her old precision had been disturbed, wronged. Now she interred the past, like a black hole in the brain. For long stretches she sat with her mouth open, and her eyes craved nothing. The wind in her voice died out. She took to bed for days that stretched to weeks when it seemed she might never get her strength back. When some days she awoke mid-afternoon and walked into the kitchen for a glass of water or slice of toast and butter, she seemed to mistrust the light even, her eyes open only to what was close at hand. Weary, insisting on being left in bed, disintegrating, she kept to herself.

One day as she was sitting under the bedcovers with a book in her lap she asked me to sweep up the dead wasps in the utility room, and I was doing that when Shelly appeared at the back door, and I noticed she'd driven her father's car and parked in the driveway. Looking for me? I said. I didn't know if you'd want to see me, she said, acknowledging we'd been at odds of late as I kept bringing up the subject of God and faith and all that, and becoming something like a dissident.

She smiled with all her teeth, pushed her hair back, and slipped a hand under the strap of her purse against her shoulder. We kissed, before I lead her into the den, her bag hanging to the floor. When we sat on the sofa, I indicated that Mother was still in bed. Shelly made a face of concern, then she pantomimed handing me a bouquet of flowers. I pretended to smell them and set them into an imaginary vase. She didn't say a word. Sitting close together, she scooted opposite of me, so that we could look at each other. Then she pushed her shoes off and rested her feet against my legs.

—She's asleep now, I said.

—I know what that's like. Has she been up at all today?

—Long enough to hand me a list of chores. Got to deal with the wasps.

Shelly's blouse exposed her smooth collarbone. She rubbed her fingers against the skin, white as wine, and looked at me with an intimate quiet. We sat like that for a few moments, bound by the dolor. The windows rattled with a cloud of wasps, and I looked around the room to see if any had got into the house. We sat on the sofa like characters in a lost play, scattered as the minutes flowed in and out of the room, as Shelly rubbed the fingernail of her right thumb against the left one, scraping off what remained of the red polish. I thought to suggest we go out over the weekend, and we began chatting about that, about meeting after work where we both had part-time jobs at the Galleria.

— You can't get beaten down.

— Do I have a choice?

— No.

We spoke of this and that until Shelly put a finger to her mouth, shushing us quiet. She went to the kitchen and came back with a glass of water and some ice, sat down next to me, shoulder to shoulder, tightened her lips and lowered her eyes. I took a sip from the glass and handed it back to her, smoothing the skin on my fingers alongside hers, until she set the water glass down and pulled her legs up to her chest on the sofa.

Outside the wasps were billowing.

Shelly was talking about needing to leave to go to dinner with her grandparents when Mother appeared in her bathrobe and slippers, shuffling into the room. She was standing stiffly, groggy, rubbing her neck as if she had an awful pain there. Her face worn, her words faint.

— Hello, sweetheart. I thought I heard your voice.

— Let me make you something, Shelly said without standing.

— No, honey, thank you.

Mother looked at me and said I'd have to find something to eat on my own, then tried to hang a smile on her mouth. She stared at the papery wasps battering against the windows as if she were blind.

All aspects of a memory, like a home, communicate to us.

The tray of cutlery in the drawer that sticks, shakers of salt and pepper on the kitchen table, magazines strewn across the sofa. It comes down to understanding something about longing. The past is the stage for the drama of that longing.

Soon as I say something like that, though, I think our lives are much too complex for so simple a characterization. It's the memory of home that's unending. Isn't it?

Your kitchen in which everyone cooks and eats and restores themselves, hallways through which everyone passes coming and going, living rooms where you visit the events of the day, and also the lost spaces—corners, window sills, empty beds, unopened cabinets, the chairs in which no one has sat alone for years. I suppose the cure, if a cure is needed, is to make your home at the center of your body, to tend to it so that you find contentment there, joyously welcoming anyone who visits, and happy, perhaps especially so, when you are, inescapably, alone.

But, is that right?

Like so many of life's memories their novelties have a tendency to wear off. The minutiae begin to pall, even to become vapid or corny. You can't quite hang onto the specter of details. For a time, they're like a long-lost relative lurking outside your door first thing in the morning, hoping to have a word. Afterward, you're ready to see them move along. Meyerland teases me with these kinds of invocations, when I get a sudden series of images in my mind. The experience of such a thing can't be imagined until it occurs. Same goes for the loss it brings. Or is it desire? We're always leaving home, and we're always returning.

Not long ago, one morning, I was starting my day in Portland inside this condition of acute awareness. I stood near the café tables outside Common Grounds, the coffee shop I go to on Hawthorne Boulevard, propped up by a fleeting ghostliness in my mind.

I heard a consoling voice in my head saying, It's structures and harmonies you're talking about.

Almost at once I felt soothed, because that voice meant all the random images ricochetting inside me must eventually cohere and, like a pain, lift. I suppose when we're forced into this awareness of affiliation, this sensation of kindredness, and all the fleeting images that shackle our wrists to the past, perhaps we are able to realize how essential it is that the foggy borderlines of memory be so tightly and meticulously defended.

For a brief moment, that morning, outside the café, on Hawthorne Boulevard, I thought of myself as wind. I imagined that, ever since I left Texas, wherever I was—at night as I drifted along the miles of streets, the houses and buildings like weeping willows whose branches spread down, or at daybreak, standing and waiting, as if all the days of my life were passing through me all at once—that I was also blowing through various other cities I've lived in, where I was always changing my ways, dodging life, escaping death. I also imagined I was the walls of all those cities, but I could not protect even myself any longer. I imagined I was constantly in mourning, asking no one to visit and comfort me and bring me peace—but I insisted on keeping the curtains open so the blue rustling sky, like waves from distant waters, could enter my rooms. I imagined sinking into those waters, a shipwreck. All around were those things that have never been dredged up. Basins and bottles and pots and chalices and flagons, covered with the seaweed—seaweed covering hunks of the old faith and rusted superstitions. I saw not one memory down there. They were too quick, like fish, to get caught in the netting. They thrashed and swam away. At last, I felt like I was nothing but a dull symbol, like the gates to a city, inside which the high buildings and underground tunnels call out to the people, as if calling out to God, *Why us?*

From the start of the walk I had the desire to remember the precise experiences that changed who I was meant to become, to contain the whole of existence inside separate episodes saturated with meaning.

But, standing on the sidewalk outside my old house, nothing was merely itself.

Another afternoon Shelly had driven over when Mother was away. This was months after the day of the wasps, in springtime. It had been raining hard for days already, pelting in streaks, drenching the houses like they were barges on an open sea until they disappeared from view. The storm's winds were turning from gray to a terrible dark silver. Muddy torrents were carved across the lawns. We sat talking in the kitchen, with the glaze of rain slanting heavily across the windows. Shelly was thumbing through stacks of folders and yellowed newspaper clippings Mother had left on the table. Inside the folders were copies of her letters of protests to presidents of companies, large and small. The correspondence included details of her experiences with that business's products or services, and often made note, for reasons hard to appreciate, her ideas about democracy or Jewish history, and always with the expectation of a refund. The clippings included articles, with inset photographs, about her volunteer work through Jewish Family Service. There was a notice on her effort to bring Soviet Jewish refugees to Houston. Another article concerned her spearheading the Harris County National Council of Jewish Woman's project to fund the newly-created *Sesame Street* for Channel 8. For a time Mother had been president of Volunteers in Public Schools, and there were materials in the folders about that. As well an article on the unusual fact of her as a female executive in the all-male waste management industry.

Shelly looked up and stared at the blurry window.

— Your mother's amazing, she said.

— She plays with live ammo, all right.

— You know what I want to know? What were you like when you were little? she said, after a pause, crossing her arms over the table and putting her head down to rest.

— Trouble. Wandering off all the time. Why? I said.

— I just wondered. Why did you wander off?

— I don't know.

— Restless?

— World traveler.

— Please, she said, lifting her head.

— What do you want me to say?

— I don't need you to say anything.

— You could run away with me.

—We're going to run away?

—Together.

—In this rain? You'll never get away. No matter how far we go. You'll bring it with you.

—You think so?

—We both would.

—We could leave all these people.

—It's possible we could be doing this, here, forever, she said, tapping her foot against my leg under the table.

—Forever? Is that possible?

—You're going to have to give up your pain one of these days.

—But I love my pain, I said.

—You don't care what people think, that's your problem. I'm good for you. You need this.

She looked at me as if something satisfying had been hard won. I watched her eyes like I was watching a drop of water drip down a windowpane, a single drop, and I waited for it to ooze down the glass, and then lengthen, and slide downward.

—Just need me to pay the bills? I said.

—I'd be very grateful, for me and the children, she said, parodying a southern belle, rolling her eyes.

—Children?

—Six.

—Six?

—You'll have to work hard. I promise, I'll have them in bed when you get home and listen to you talk about the office and advise you, then up at five to get the children off and out of your way. How's that?

—Really?

—Hmmm-hmmm. Do you know what you want from us? she said.

—This is what I want. You shouldn't feel responsible for everything, I said, waving a hand between us, and we sat quietly after that, listening to the rain falling in shattered knocks on the roof.

—Must be hard, not feeling responsible.

—Not really.

—I want us to be something to hold on to.

—To possess?

—To hold onto. Not to feel hurt.

—Am I hurting you?

—No, I don't mean that. I just want to keep this. What do you want?

—I don't want to hurt you. What I want is to run out into the rain and see what happens. That's all I mean, I said.

—And then?

—No idea.

—And never mind we might drown?

—We know how to swim. Is that your fear?

—And that's a life?

I could hear what she was saying, but I was less worried about getting the point than I was holding onto my instinctive ambition, holding it, like smoke, inside my lungs. Did I truly think she embodied what I thought of as a possible future—in Texas, in Meyerland, my Meyerland Domesticus? When our time came abruptly to an end, on a winter day, when all across the city leaves were disappearing off branches and swimming in the wind across the air, we stood in the little foyer of her father's house, and I said I didn't know how to preserve this thing. I went on and on about it, about how I couldn't burrow myself in Meyerland ("You're stubborn, that's why"), about how I hadn't one nerve ending left ("You don't?"), about how I needed to find a new mold to exist in. I wore her out with the severity of my insistence, even though I also wished it could have been managed differently and that I was not, for better or for worse, a deserter. One stretch she held the silence between us by looking down at the floor. We both would give all this up, she said finally, if it meant we could have one more day the way it was before, before everything. One more day, but we can't. That's our life, she said. We hardly spoke to each other again.

Back in the kitchen, that afternoon of the storm, Shelly and

I heard clanging from the street and ran outside to stand on the porch under the awning. Two neighbors were dragging a red canoe over the pavement to where the water was already deep enough for them to put in. They mounted the canoe and paddled toward Manhattan Street shouting and laughing. We waved to greet them since we were the only people outside. Under the hoods of their bright jackets dripping with rain they nodded back. The canoe bobbed through the water. Once they had gone, I slipped my hands against Shelly's back, against her skin, lightly pressing into her. We turned and stepped inside and sat in the den for a long time, silent as wind. She untied a ribbon from her hair, slowly, and her hair fell around her shoulders. As if I were removing her dress I leaned over and eased some of the black strands from around her eyes. It was like time was floating down to the floor. We could hear each other breathe all the way to the edges of our breaths.

Under a soft blanket we lay side by side, and kissed, and the silence of that rainy afternoon fell over our eyes, in thin drops. My heart felt comforted, as if we were reducing ourselves to nothing of what we had ever been. I could feel the small pillow against my head, the skin on our arms touching the way shadows touch. An imaginary spirit engraved itself across our bodies. Whatever mistakes the world had made against us were absent. Far off, a low thunder under black clouds unfurled nothing at all, followed by the hush of stillness. We held close, experiencing something like the mutual pleasure of submission without the pleasure of mastery. And yet it was good to have even that feeling, as if our future pleasures were being held in trust. When I reached over to touch her, to smooth my fingers down her bare arms, to press our skin together, our flaws were in sync, underlying the mishaps and uncertainties, side by side with the feeling that we both knew what we were invoking from each other and tried to savor that. Solemnity took over. Which one of us, I wonder now, kept waiting for the other to lay bare something more?

Hiding from the thunder and rain, brushing the hair from

our eyes, out of breath, we were the simplest versions of ourselves. What flaws we offered dropped away with every drawing breath. We sought and then overcame the unbearable, needing each other's admiration. We weren't looking to free ourselves from being, we knew that much. Shelly did. To preserve her shyness was a simple glowing in the room. Her silence was a form of order. Every touch of my fingers to her skin, and her fingers to mine, did more than we wanted it to and also less than we wanted it to. The sensual we took seriously, and that was the beauty of it. What I didn't want to believe was that being with her was an accident, like everything else, or that all sense of what I knew of myself wasn't true. Soon we drifted to sleep, is all, as if it was better for some things in life to remain incomprehensible, indecipherable.

The next day was the quarrel with the rabbi.

Texas

A home need not have a meaning, and, like most things in nature, often doesn't.

If home isn't where we are, is it who we are? In spite of how often we've moved from one place to another, how alert we are to identity and community, however we navigate our economic positions, we do recognize the importance of place. Now, when people ask where I'm from, I usually say, Oregon. But the word I mean is, Texas.

What's the difference between the enigma of one designation or another?

As soon as I write down that question, I realize the answer holds the paradox of home. Doesn't it?

A home reveals the inexpressible sources of life in its particulars.

The day I arrived in Meyerland was months before Hurricane Harvey brought more than fifty inches of rain over Houston. In addition to Beth Israel taking on three feet of water from flooding, with four feet lapping the sides of the building, the ground floor of the Jewish Community Center flooded in ten feet of water. I'd read that sewage flooded Beth Yeshurun's sanctuary, as much as four feet high in some places. Nearly every one of the thousand plush seats would have to be replaced. The synagogue would be stripped to the floorboards and studs. Torahs were saved, but thousands of prayer books were destroyed. Historic papers stained. Carpeting, wooden doors, furniture—all of it had to be discarded. Beth Yeshurun's

High Holidays that fall were held at Lakewood, the Christian mega-church, at the invitation of their charismatic pastor, Joel Osteen. I'd learned that, in the Beth Yeshurun cemetery on Allen Parkway, floodwaters rose to the tops of the headstones. Two months after Harvey on a sunny Sunday in October, congregants gathered to bury two thousand prayer books in a *g'nizah*, so that all the books with divine names, spoiled in the flood, were given a respectful burial. It's an ancient tradition for ruined, sacred documents to be hidden away. Perhaps some day, long in the future, scholars will dig up the Hurricane Harvey *g'nizah* to identify and study what was concealed there.

But none of that had happened yet.

Late in the afternoon, when I walked into the cavernous sanctuary under the dimmed lights at Beth Yeshurun, and the doors hushed behind me, and I could hear a machine hum of air conditioning, the moment felt like stepping gingerly into a familiar bath. But also like I was slipping underwater and then swimming back to the surface to a place that had been waiting for me for thousands and thousands of years.

Above the bimah hung the Eternal Lamp, with gold dove's wings. In the center of the white curtain of the Holy Ark—a five-meters long curtain that hung like a fluttering robe from ceiling to floor—there was emblazoned an embroidered gold crown, with the Hebrew words, *keter-torah*, The Crown of the Torah.

I thumbed through the synagogue's paper bulletin and noted an upcoming class on Jewish Justices on the US Supreme Court. There was scheduled a presentation on Children of Abraham: Muslim-Jewish Dialogue. On Friday night, the third through fifth graders from the Day School would be singing during services.

I walked past the spare yarmulke bin. From the front of the sanctuary, on the bimah, I stood behind the lectern and fingered several yellow sticky notes scrawled with announcements of upcoming events and the names of congregants the rabbis had visited in the hospitals that week and for whom they wanted to offer a prayer. Facing the empty rows and the thousand empty seats, I imagined the sanctuary filled with people, all of us pulling in our breaths all at once, sharing the one breath that I had known before. I imagined all those fading class pictures I stood in on the bimah, the students arranged by height, the big hair and wide glasses and pimpled faces, braces, and crooked smiles, and stoney eyes, year after year, from kindergarten and grade school, all the way through high school Torah classes, each year the portraits reprinted in the *Jewish Herald Voice*. I turned to face the Holy Ark, arrayed with the first Hebrew words of each of the Ten Commandments. Without hesitation I pressed the electronic button, shaped like a doorbell, to part the splendor of the curtains that concealed a dozen cloth-covered, silver crowned Torahs, each embroidered with shields, etched with engraved images of lions holding up the Ark of the Covenant, and insignias for the Twelve Tribes of Israel. Resting on a shelf was a lanky *yad*, its silver finger meant for following the text during the Torah readings now pointing at nothing.

Behind the Torahs was a stained-glass motif of the Burning Bush.

Near the back of the sanctuary, I took a seat in the dark. The tune to the prayer *Ein Keloheinu* came into my head. It's a mystical meditation about how none compares to God, meant to bring about an ecstatic vision. I opened the siddur and rubbed my fingers along the words of the Mourner's Kaddish, and I recoiled at the thought of God as a holy name beyond any expression of gratitude ever spoken in the world.

A teenage boy with short black hair, tennis shorts, and a tee shirt, alongside a woman in an untucked denim shirt rolled at the sleeves, entered through the hushed doors of the sanctuary with a fresh calm, both wearing yarmulkes. From the ark they brought down one of the scrolls, wrapped with a white cover. She showed the boy how to remove the cover and set it down on a bench, called him Daniel, and asked for the *chumash* he was carrying, to help her find the spot to practice his bar mitzvah Torah portion. Under my breath I hummed the aliyah, the prayer that introduces the recitation.

Here, found it, said the teacher. Start here. *Vya-yesh*. See it? I'll practice to call you up, and you say, you respond, Amen. Into the microphone he chanted in a voice that sounded like a scratchy crop report turned low in the next room. I pictured the gnarled Hebrew letters on the parchment reaching out to each other, one by one, like a circle of men and women holding hands.

OK, stop, the teacher said. Stop here. I just want to remind you. it's *Va-ya-vet*. Say it. *Va-ya-vet*. Try it four times, she instructed.

He repeats her, and resumes, chanting louder this time, moves easily through the parts, stumbles, corrects himself. His voice breaks on the high notes. Can you go back a few words and try again? the teacher stops him again. Good. Torah means teaching. Did you know that? she asks. Daniel shakes his head. Torah refers to the scroll, but also to what is inside, she says. The text has neither vowels nor punctuation. Right? That's because when you chant it aloud, you convey its meaning, she says. Do it again. And he picks up where he left off, singing the flubbed parts, with her pleasantly correcting him.

Far as I could tell neither of them had noticed me in the last rows of the sanctuary. I closed my eyes and listened to Daniel sustain his grim monotone. What was astonishing was how it felt like I was experiencing other people's religion, as if I were a man from centuries in the future transported to this place to discover what was going on here. It was like I had discovered ancient artifacts and bones from a cave once covered in a great flood.

What is this mystery that makes people bow to it? This place as evidence of people asking for understanding and devoting themselves to it so they can continue to know it? To be inspired, to aspire, to be fascinated, and to recreate Torah every day through which people will live and grow and reinhabit the mystery, and then to recognize that consciousness of it? As I had secretly felt when I was a boy, I began to think it was me who was sick. How else could I have sought some other self kept hidden, or who I took to be my true self, who was not deluded even when no one was around?

But also, at the same time, as if I were I putting on a familiar hat, so many of the old meanings descended. I pictured myself like the earliest patriarchs—like Adam I was kicked out of the garden, like Cain I lived a life of wandering, like the people who built the Tower of Babel my profane act sent me scattering, like the uprooted Abraham and the hungry Joseph I set out on a quest for new land. Perhaps I am most like Jacob, a man of impulses, the outsider, always mobile, on the run, with zigzagging efficiency, eyes on the horizon, who turned his back on his relationships left behind. As with Jacob's series of departures, my departure from Texas was urgent, tethered to a betrayal. Like Jacob, I set out for anonymity. Like Jacob, I have felt a sense of internal displacement from a place and from the people.

Unlike Jacob, I have not seen God face to face. Nor have I sought to. Not yet.

The streets of Meyerland all these years have been like the bones of a former life, an heirloom I carry in a wooden box from city to city. From thousands of miles away, when I hold the bones and look at them in my hands, I feel the sense of a big humid sky, and I link to all that I left behind, all that I unwelcomed myself to. I made it, I say to the bones. I broke free to the last breath. Good for you, the bones say. Do what you're going to do, say the bones. Then the bones add, God will take care of the rest.

I crossed my legs, let my thoughts drift, and remembered the night Shelly Rose and I had arrived at the Galleria Hotel for an Esquires banquet. Her in a blue, strapless dress, me in a double-breasted suit like I was some kind of detective. 1981. We were in high school, and I'd been asked, as a past president, to give a speech, something like a sermon.

The banquet was smaller than in the past, a few dozen couples was all. Everything was decorated Israeli blue, including the table cloths. I looked out at the guys and girls dressed in coats and ties, formal dresses, shining and coifed, baby-cheeked, as if they had brushed their faces along with their hair. What all the kids reflected in their suits and long dresses with spaghetti straps, boutonnieres, nosegays, and the officers in rented tuxedos from Al's Formal Wear in Braeswood Square, was something of a Texas illusion. Some were shouting, others saying nothing. I felt repulsed, disappointed with myself. The boys seemed obsessively sincere, a little cozy. I wondered, as I looked at them all as they sat straight up in their seats at the banquet tables with their tall, magnificent dates, fiddling with their napkins, the silverware gleaming surreally, white plates empty, was: Am I the only one asking, why are we doing this?

I adjusted the microphone and began speaking slowly with a sinewy drawl, telling a story from shul about a man who took great care with his garden. He was constantly working at building a beautiful garden, I said. All over was the sweet smell of trees dazed with sunlight, a solitary willow tree, pansies and clover, brown-eyed daisies, climbing roses that twisted next to honeysuckle, fat creamy tulips. Even in autumn, when the sun was shining flat and low the way it does, there was little sadness in that garden. Instead there was harmony and hope. There were so many rocks and stones underneath the dirt that the man worked for years removing the stones and flinging them one by one into the street. Over time a wall of discarded stones built up between his garden and the street. The wall was ten feet high, covered with moss and ivy. One day a passerby asked the man why he threw so many stones into the street. He answered that the house and garden were his and the stones were in the way. Besides on the other side of the wall is just the street and that has nothing to do with me. The passerby looked at the man who built the garden and, before walking away, said only that nothing is permanent.

Tonight, I said, after I paused to let this portion of the sermon sink in, when I think of that story, I feel a lot like the man who built that garden. I said, for years everybody put a lot into building Esquires, this seed for the garden of the Jewish community in Texas. A lot of guys built up the club and stayed in it until the end, so Esquires stayed on top. As older guys left the club when the time came, newcomers came forward, asking little in return, tending the garden and the road to it. My friends, tonight I say to you, *Sa-lah-lah-me-ka al-pe-nay-ha-ma-yim, kee-bay-rov hay-ya-mim teem-zah-ay-nu.* "Cast your bread upon the waters, for after many days you will find it." Are you ready tonight to commit once again to the values of history and tradition so that others can experience them, here, in the Promised Land of Texas? Our lives are not just dances and having a banquet, or hanging out at a sweetheart's house after school, as fun as that is. Before any of us became members, people had developed the foundations of a club like Esquires upon the foundations of Jewish values. Upon handing the club down to us, they knew we would continue developing it according to those values. We in turn, you in turn, hand it down to others, confident that the traditions will go on. Tonight I call on you to rise up. Rise up for brotherhood and commitment. Rise up and become a foundation of Jewish life here in Texas.

The teenagers stared at me, as if bombarded, and hardly applauded. Shelly seemed to be holding her breath, and offered a shrug when I sat down.

When the ceremony was over, and the dance started, she whispered that some of the parents wanted to talk to me, and I should walk among the crowd, shaking hands. A DJ spun the music. Kids were dancing. Did I, that night, believe even one word of what I had said?

—You have a real future in this community, Frank Karkowsky's father said, shaking my hand, and I could feel his sharp wedding band against my fingers.

—That was an inspired talk, the father of one of the new officers said, asking about my father's health, and promising that everything was going to be OK in my life if I kept on like this, patting my shoulder, then pressing his business card inside the breast pocket of my coat.

—These kids won't get it tonight, but they will later. I hear you haven't joined BBYO, is that right? his wife said, shaking my hand with both of hers, then hugging Shelly who was urging me forward, like a glassy vibration, pressing her hand to my elbow.

—True. No. I haven't joined, I said.

—We all need to hear those words. We all need to be reminded from time to time. Oh, honey, you look so much like your mother, she said to Shelly and kissed her on the cheek.

The DJ was playing "Maggie May." Couples were slow-dancing behind us. They appeared to be lost, the boys with bright shirts starched around their skinny white necks, the girls with long hair and shiny dresses, all of them shuffling against each other in the ballroom, skin to skin, before the shortest boys started chasing each other around the room, and all that was left on the dance floor were barefooted girls dancing.

On the slow drive home along North Braeswood, Shelly sat very still, staring at the road. The windows were down, and we could feel the wind blink across the streetlights and blur our faces. It was the kind of breeze that made you wistful. The foliage of the elms and oaks and sycamores rustled overhead, no two alike, in good times and in bad, with the roots keeping to their own laws.

—Why did you do that? You were just supposed to congratulate them for a good term. I mean, I agree with you. Everything you said. I wish you had given a different speech. Not so tough. I'm tired. I want to curl up and watch TV, she said.

I didn't answer. I also hadn't told her about the invitation to a small party that night with guys I knew from school. They weren't Jewish, but that wasn't it. There was going to be beer and pot, and she didn't go for that sort of thing. We wriggled out of the car outside her house, and I walked her to the door to say goodnight. On the walkway, she bent forward at the waist, then straightened up and flipped her hair back over her head, her face flush and shining, like she was a bird that had just landed in the grass. Above us the black sky seemed to be moving like water. It was a sky nobody else could have dreamed up while here and there low clouds twirled and disappeared.

Driving alone on the South Loop to the party, with the windows rolled down, I could feel the city quivering. A humid wind clung to the skyscrapers and office towers in the distance with their lights burning forever. Cruising seventy-five with the rest of the traffic past empty apartment complexes lining the feeder roads, listening to KIKK, the country station, I passed the Astrodome and manufacturing warehouses, and took in the odor of gas and exhaust. I was pinned to the driver's seat, the lights of the freeway filling the dashboard with alternating brightness and dark. The week before, Reichstein, Lerner, and I got together for the first time in many months, long after we'd been officers together in Esquires. We met to shoot pool at the Jewish Community Center. Check it out, I said, when we greeted each other, and I showed them the used blue jean jacket with warm lining I was wearing that I'd found at a thrift store in Galveston. Reichstein was chalking his stick, wiping his hands clean onto the tail of his white polo shirt, and he hit the balls like he was stirring food on a stove. Lerner distorted his face before each shot, figuring the angle and shape of it, clopping around the table in flip-flops. He was wearing a bright, lemon-colored button-down. I was no better at playing pool, slamming each ball, not thinking about leaving myself lined up for the next shot except by chance. The guys were talking about BBYO and their new high school Jewish fraternity club. They were talking about kicking out some of the new members. They didn't fit, Reichstein said. We had this epic party, Lerner said, where people talked about who they disliked as loud as they could and those guys got the message.

—Who are they? What was wrong with them? I asked.

—They didn't fit. Corner pocket, Lerner said, leaning his stomach against the table to aim the white ball at a solid.

I watched the two of them circle the table, striking the

solids and stripes, the cue ball ricocheting against the sides and rolling to a peculiar stop on the green felt. I wondered about the implications of their new enthusiasm. Perhaps I thought it seemed distasteful, diminishing. They began talking about the differences between the BBYO clubs in Meyerland and the ones in Memorial, an upscale neighborhood near downtown where a cluster of Jewish families also lived. The guys seemed pleased with the mystique of their new order.

—You can change your mind and join, Lerner said.

—I'm a refusenik.

—Fuck that. Before long we could be in charge again.

—I'm not going to kick people out.

Lerner coughed out a laugh. Reichstein squeaked his stick into a cube of chalk.

All the way to Mark Solis' house, out to where the Loop merges with the South Freeway, I drove with little purpose but to forget the failure of the sermon. The night ahead would mark the end of my first education and the beginning of my future one—when I pushed open the door and stepped directly into the living room. I could feel cool air. There was an aroma of pork and spices, salsa, avocados. What smelled like chili. But no one in the kitchen. In the backyard was talking and a boombox turned low, and when I stepped onto the concrete patio, I appeared like a boat everyone was expecting come late to the dock.

—The party's here, shouted Solis, who stood to give me a hug, then flicked at his thin, black mustache.

Barrel-chested, with trim brown hair, in shorts and tee shirt, and flip-flops, stooping a little, his face bright and his eyes nearly shut, he directed me to four guys sitting in lawn chairs on the patio, a rickety table in the center of them with a red bong on top, smoke puffing out. Next to that a red frisbee with shake from the marijuana scattered inside the rim. Bags of potato chips. Silver cans of Lone Star beer.

—You on your own?

—I am.

—Your old lady?

—Gone home.

I went around the circle, nodding and high-five-ing. Will Cozort was a straight-haired kid who had once quieted English class by speaking eloquently about the dreams of Christian believers after we read Dante's *Inferno*. Scott Sullivan, president of our class, once told me he smiled all the time in school because teachers trusted smiling kids, and then they wouldn't know he was a stoner. Kevin Bragdon I'd only met once before outside of school. Jed Dennis, who I admired as the smartest kid in our grade, liked to talk about George Orwell.

—We're living *1984* right now. You don't believe me? You're Winston Smith. We all are, he said once as we walked to lunch during a break from Ms. Lyles's English class.

—At least we get Julia, I said.

—Joke if you want to. Reagan is Stalin.

I drew closer to them all and sat on the grass on the edge of the patio, flicking two ants from my leg. Not all the guys were smoking pot.

—Pass him the bong. My mijo is due. You wearing a three-piece suit? You look like Sam Spade. Miguel Vargas, or something.

—Careful, Meyerland, that's some strong shit. You party, right? Bragdon asked.

I nodded.

—When was your first time?

—I stole a joint from under my oldest brother's bed. He kept his dope in a shoebox, I said and grabbed hold of the bong, but the ice had melted, so I took a slow drag, and held my breath.

—What happened? Bragdon asked and I started talking while holding my breath, the smoke clambering across my lungs.

—I crawled under the bed to get the shoebox and suddenly he appeared inside the room and blocked the door. Figures you'd steal the fattest one, he says, so I handed it back to him. Then he goes, You can have the shake. That's it. But you got to ask.

I lifted my head back to hold the smoke in longer, and pushed it out through my teeth, I watched the wisps rise in the humid air toward the few stars you could see in the night sky. Solis fingered the boombox and put in a cassette. Guitars, accordion.

—Who's this? asked Sullivan, reaching for the plastic case.

—Freddy Fender, dude. Baldemar Huerta, Solis said.

Bragdon took the bong. With a paper clip, he stabbed at the silver stem, then rested a fat green bud in the pipe, lit up, and inhaled hard so we could hear the water bubble.

—"Wasted Days and Wasted Nights." "Until the Last Teardrop Falls." Swamp pop, amigo, Tejano, Bragdon said through his held breath as Sullivan rolled onto his side in the grass and stretched his legs out and read the liner notes.

Dennis was talking in a quiet drawl to Cozort about what he kept calling a General Theory of Our Lady of Oblivion, and waved me over to listen. His voice was warm, like old cedar.

—First you lose your eyesight. Try it. Close your eyes. Do it. Only see shadows, am I right? Everything else is confusion. You cling to the walls of your brain, that's what you're doing. You struggle in the starlight. You can't find any way to magnify the last thought in your brain. You can taste the air burning. That's your family, man. Sí?

—Sí.

—Your mother and father. Sí?

—Sí.

—Uncles and aunts. You're going mad now. Then you see a donkey dancing on the rooftop of a house next door. I ask you, is that an illusion? You see it. Don't you? I can see it. It makes me weak. Like my eyesight is shot. Now you can start finding incredible things. Mistakes you can fix.

—How do you fix them? asked Cozort.

—You catch those hummingbirds behind your closed eyes, man. See them?

—Jellyfish, I said, holding my eyes closed.

—That's right, man. Hummingbirds that become jellyfish.

A haze of happy nights when the sun ambles down to Australia and New Zealand and Papua New Guinea. And the phantoms rest their heads right in your lap.

I opened my eyes and could see that Cozort and Dennis were shut-eyed, nodding their whole bodies to the music. Rising quietly, walking into the kitchen where Solis was turning off the stove, I felt spurred, jolted, like there was something un-suffering in my head.

—I am your people, Solis said with a whispery persistence, stirring the pot of chili, fixing his gaze right on my eyes.

—You make all this?

—My mom. She'll be back later. What's with you now? You OK? High?

Outside, Freddy Fender had been turned up. Sullivan was two-stepping with an invisible partner and moved his body awkwardly like a shirt waving in the wind on a clothesline. Dennis was standing against the side of the house with his arms folded, one leg bent up with the flat of his heel on the siding, absolutely still, like he was waiting for a department store to open. Cozort had rolled onto his side and was reading out loud from a dog-eared copy of *One Flew Over the Cuckoo's Nest*.

—'Tis, indeed, said Bragdon to some passage I couldn't hear.

—Piss on your fucking rules! Wait till we tell Ms. Lyles about tonight! drawled Dennis.

Solis pulled a cigarette from a pack he had in his shirt pocket and lit it up.

—Could you imagine, she'd start breathing heavy, her face would swell, her lips turn white. "Ken Kesey is the merry prankster," she'd say, and we'd say, "Whoa, Madame L., slow down, M'Lady, feel for it. It's K.K. It's Kenny the K. Old cuckoo's nest. Cuckoo! I'm coo-coo for Cocoa Puffs!" Solis sang, lighting up.

—She only wants you to interpret it the way she does, Sullivan said.

—A five-paragraph essay can't be junk. Junk is for fools, I

said, imitating her thick drawl.

—Junk is for fools! Bragdon whispered and picked up the bong.

—Kesey's right, man. We all hide who we are. I don't know who I am, Dennis said.

—Bong hits help, said Bragdon.

—Not arbitrary, man. You got roped into being who you think you are, Sullivan said, sitting up and waving his hands.

We went on like that, passing the bong, discussing whether you're roped or chained or handcuffed, what was dominant in society and what never came close to being understood.

—Where you been earlier? Bragdon asked, pressing his fingers against the open collar of my suit.

I explained Esquires, the topic of my speech, and I felt my Jewish inheritance as something defined and defining. But I also felt like a ghost sneaking into someone else's life, even if it was my own.

—You gave a sermon? You going to be a rabbi? he said, choking out smoke from another bong hit, coughing and spitting and trying to speak, slapping his hand against his thigh.

—I did.

—How many people?

—I don't know. A few dozen. Used to be bigger. A lot bigger.

—All dressed like that?

—Plus formal dresses for the girls. And corsages.

—You gave a sermon about the importance of Jewishism? Dennis said.

—It's called Judaism, Solis said.

—I know that, I'm kidding. Just kidding. You gave a sermon about the necessity of right honorable Jewish living, with corsages?

—And boutonnières, I said.

—Fucking flowers coming out everyone's ass. And you give your tribe your philosophical views on being God-loving and God-fearing?

—That's the Baptists, I said.

—God cock-sucking with a beanie on your head, and now you're here getting baked with us children of Confederate crackers?

—And one Hispanic, I said, pointing at Solis.

—I'm Chicano, said Solis, taking a drag on his cigarette.

—I thought you were Mexican, said Bragdon.

—Tejano, amigo.

—And one patriot of the Mexican people, a Catholic descendent of the defeat of General Antonio Lopez De Santa Anna at the Battle of San Jacinto, I said, and we all laughed, except Bragdon.

—Fuck you, people, I'm not in all your fucking International Baccalaureate bullshit classes. Give me that bong. I'm dirt. I'm East Texas dirt. It's all the way up my ass.

I threw an arm around Solis's neck.

—You are in the company of Texans, my friends. You are witnesses to situational irony. I'm blowing bowls with you lovers of Christ, after wagging my fat, peasant finger at my tribal dudes, all under the secret cover of the worldwide Jewish conspiracy. Tell that to Ms. Lyles. Tell that to Ronald Reagan.

—Do you contradict yourself? Do you contain multitudes? whispered Solis, imitating Ms. Lyles when she quoted Walt Whitman.

We began drinking mouthfuls of beer, and talked about football and swamp music, clean-cut types, dirty hippies, the Civil War, girls from school, teachers we liked, and novels. Each idea we offered at first darkened, then turned to gold, in the uproarious gab that carried on until morning. It could not have occurred to me, talking about books and music and drugs, that I was now a young man hurtling into the air into unknown weather. I must have known the sky would not fall. I would not be left paralyzed or murdered by a thief. Snakes would not twist around my neck. Nor would an angel arrive in the night to fracture my leg. Nor would I be asked to murder my son.

Departing the main sanctuary, I left Daniel and his teacher behind, and I wandered in the empty corridors of the shul alongside walls of Chagall-like portraits: Noah's ark, the binding of Isaac, Jacob in the land of the people of the East when he meets Rachel with her sheep at the well, Moses parting the Red Sea.

Walking down the hallway right then came an older gentleman. Thin and pale in a black pull-over, slacks, and sneakers, he held in his palm a step-count pedometer that clicked with each step. His gait was misshapen. The florescent light shined on his black yarmulke. In the bright light of the hallway it was just the two of us. He looked to be in his eighties, lithe, quiet-faced, his hair a neutral ash. He had rounded his shoulders, as if to stay warm, which gave him a meditative mien. From down the hallway, from where I was standing, every feature of his face became familiar.

It was Rabbi Segal, now an old man.

What an impossible coincidence, precisely the sort of thing you'd leave out if this were fiction.

He appeared to speak, but turned down a corridor and kept with his pace, stepping and clicking, then slipped behind a wall like a skiff, vaulted and cracked, through the brightly lit interior. With the metallic click of the step-count pedometer preceding him, he reappeared, nodded, looked away, and crossed toward the Day School. Then he looked back, squinting, and held my eyes. Are you looking for someone? he said in a voice that was tattered but unobstructed, keeping his pace, not intending to stop, beads of sweat on his brow, clicking his counter. No, sir, I said, before he walked on and disappeared behind another corridor.

I was surprised and not surprised, curious, almost unbelieving, the synchronicity, the two of us like ancient frigates that happened upon each other out of the fog in a calm current.

I have long thought that the only way for me to live in Texas is to believe nothing and to live somewhere else.

Which is what I was thinking when I hustled into the little Orthodox chapel to consider what it was I might say to Rabbi Segal, now that we were, after nearly forty years, face to face. It wasn't like I could just walk up to him as he kept his pace and clicked his pedometer and go, So, rabbi, as I was saying.

What I didn't know at that moment, while I waited inside the empty chapel to gather my thoughts, taking in the surroundings, the small Holy Ark filled with several Torahs, narrow aisles of seats, stacks of black prayer books, is that the following morning, Saturday, on Shabbat, I would return and slip into the Orthodox service inside that same little chapel. I'd intended to stay a half hour, take notes, is all. But when I eyed the back row for an open seat behind what I figured to be about seventy people, a woman's voice called my name.

It was Marilyn Hassid, one of my grade school teachers from the Day School, waving me over to sit beside her. A shine in her smile, skepticism in her eyes, she was dressed in a dark purple dress with a white shawl, painterly gray in her dark hair. I put two fingers to my forehead like a headache was coming on, turned to grab a black yarmulke from the wooden bin, and borrowed a tallit from the rack—twirling the white garment around my shoulders without saying the prayer about how God is exalted and that I am garbed in his splendor.

She motioned me over. patting the empty seat next to her, inviting me to sit with her friends, a group of women I didn't recognize. We embraced. Directly in front of us an ashen-haired man stood, davening loudly. Others followed under an archipelago of yarmulkes—striped, knitted, white silk, black silk, blue with gold trim, blue with silver stitching, black with silver stars, even one in the orange and white colors of the University of Texas. Here the congregants were being asked to list people in need of remembrance, with individuals calling out their Hebrew names.

The Torah portion got underway. The reading, as it happened, was from Genesis 32, when Jacob, returning from exile, frightened and distressed, about to meet his brother Esau for the first time after many years estranged, fears Esau will strike him down for stealing his birthright, and prays to the Lord who had instructed him to return to his homeland. The night before, along the banks of the Jabbok River, Jacob dreams of wrestling with an angel of the Lord until the break of dawn.

Of all the portions, I thought, the one time I return to Beth Yeshurun, it's Genesis 32. It's the sort of coincidence, yet again, a novelist would have to cut.

One of the things about all this that troubles me is the Jewish idea that a return to faith is always possible for those who have strayed or pointedly rebelled. Staying is a Jewish act, leaving is a Jewish act, and returning is a Jewish act. The journey of return is known as *teshuvah*. Its essence can be found in the Book of Hosea: "O Israel, return unto the Lord thy God; for thou hast fallen by thine iniquity."

But how can one return if acknowledging God's existence is of no interest, and therefore becoming a servant of the Lord, submitting to God's jurisdiction, and abiding by God's commands, is of no interest?

The counter-argument goes, to yield to God is to proclaim one's freedom from human servitude. No returnee to God, no penitent, ought to imagine that he is too remote from righteousness on account of his past sins and transgressions.

C'mon. It wasn't a sin. It was a choice.

I followed the chanting, but the story was a mess. In the ancient narratives, a name reveals the character of a person. The knowledge of the name of a person has dimensions of mystery and power. The angel refuses to give Jacob his name, yet he blesses him. It wasn't long before I was thinking how the questions of identity, revealing of names, and the sought-after blessing in Genesis 32 echo the episode from a few chapters earlier, where Jacob seizes Esau's rightful birthright by deceiving their blind father Isaac and claiming his brother's blessing.

The wrestling with the angel in Genesis 32 is a paraphrase of the motifs from the earlier scene of deception. This time, in the dream, Jacob discovers his true identity. On the other hand, because the fight is never completed, the wrestling truly never ends. We're to take it that one's identity is a work in progress.

I could feel the borrowed tallit tight over my shoulders, the soft strings of the tzitzit at my fingertips when the sermon began—Shabbat Shalom! called a young red-headed rabbi I didn't recognize—and he characterized the morning's portion in Genesis 32 as a cliffhanger, like an old Hollywood serial called, Jacob and Esau Meet Again. Stay tuned to see if Jacob gets killed!

Why stay tuned? Everybody read this chapter last year. And the year before. And the year before that for three thousand years. We know what happens. He doesn't get killed.

Y'akov is renamed Israel, the red-headed rabbi was saying, and therefore he can now seek forgiveness. A Jew, he goes on, when seeking forgiveness, is obliged to compensate the victim. An eye for an eye with something of commensurate value. In Jewish law, said the rabbi, when you ask forgiveness, the victim must forgive. For both, it is an act of turning away from one's former self and becoming a renewed self: *Teshuva* plus *sh'leesha*, he says. Faith is put in humanity and not God. Faith that people can change.

Isn't it strange, I whispered to Marilyn, that even though Jacob's hip has been dislocated, the angel is the one who has to ask Jacob to release him? She whispered back, And no one ever talks about the rape of Dinah when we do these chapters either.

I noticed a bulge beneath a congregant's tallit a few rows in front of us and pointed it out to her. Is that what I think it is? Yes, she whispered, he's packing—even some rabbis in the Orthodox shuls in town carry guns. You can tell who's carrying a gun because they wear a pin shaped like a menorah in their lapel, she said. Texas Jews with guns, I said, where do they think we are, the West Bank?

She raised an eyebrow at the words, *West Bank*. At one time,

I might have pounced on that raised eyebrow and retorted something about the need to give up the American Jewish guilt for escaping Europe before the Second World War, to give up feeling inferior to Israeli Jews, to give up ceding moral authority to the Israeli government, and I remembered right then the snide remark I made to my mother, all those years ago, on the day of the quarrel, Yiddish, no, nukes, yes.

But to Marilyn, in my retirement, I demurred. OK, OK, I said, Judea, and winked.

The last prayers picked up in a mumble of southern accents.

Before the Torah was returned to its cradle in the ark, an usher in suit and tie and a rosy face, came over and leaned next to me to ask if I'd like, as a guest that morning, to open the ark for the return of the Torah. Thank you, I said, adjusting my tallit, but someone else should enjoy the honor. He had intended to shake my hand, but pulled back.

Standing silently inside the empty Orthodox chapel, late on Friday afternoon, the day before, I decided to leave the building quietly. But when I stepped into the hallway, the rabbi was waiting, with his hands folded, resting them in front of his waist. He was nodding, gently squinting, as if trying to deflect a glare.

—Rabbi?

As if whoever he thinks I am, like a pillar of smoke, is forming in his mind, he bobbed his head. I stepped close to shake his hand. His skin soft as plush.

I said my name.

—Yes. That's it. I remember. I remember. Here you are, he said in a quivery voice, with a nod of the head, lips pursed and wet, eyes half open, and he took a step backward to regard what it is he's seeing.

We talked about his family, his grandchildren, and where I was living now in Oregon. He asked about my brothers and my parents. Easy talk. I explained the reason I was at the shul that day, looking around, working on a book, and asked if he had a minute for a question or two.

—Sure, sure. You remember the place? Do you? You know, I've written some books, he said.

—I've read your books.

—I self-publish them. It's okay. I like doing it.

—Do you remember you used to lead an Exodus reenactment? Remember? The children of Israel crossing the bayou?

—Near *Pesach*. Yes. A lot of families.

—We walked from the shul to the JCC. Is that right? Or was it the other way?

—No. Right. From here to the Center. You know why? The Men's Club was very active in those days. They hosted the bagels and lox after the Exodus. Remember? Fellas said to me, they said they'd only do it if they could set up early at the Center. And while we were on the walk from the shul, they could take a shvitz beforehand. Did you know that?

As though he had all the time in the world the rabbi folded his arms and looked like he was ready for the next question, whatever angle I might come from.

—Do you remember you carried a long wooden staff? A shepherd's crook?

—That's right.

—I always wondered, where'd you get that? Do you still have it?

—I don't know. Someone gave that to me. I don't know.

—Another question? May I? Your first High Holidays here was 1973. Do you remember?

—No. That was not my first. No. I was here before that.

—I mean, your first as head rabbi, I said, mentioning Rabbi Malev, who served as senior rabbi for decades before dying in the summer of 1973.

—That's right. In July. Rabbi Malev died in July. You have a good memory.

—I wanted to ask you about your relationship with him.

Were you close?

—No. Not especially.

—I've read that he didn't appreciate a survey you did with Jewish female college students, or something, about the sexual practices of young women. What was that about?

—That was my doctoral study. I spoke about the results of that survey during Shabbat once. Made a lot of people uncomfortable. But I wanted to shake things up. Is that all?

—Did you like being rabbi here? A lot of trouble. No? According to your books, I mean.

—A little bit of light pushes away a lot of darkness, he said, and seemed to be searching my eyes, moving closer to listen, close enough I could smell the sweat on his skin mixed with cologne, before he sought to regain an amicable look, and he appeared ready to walk away.

—One more thing. May I?

—Of course. Ask. Go ahead, he said, wriggling his fingers.

There was nothing to be gained, and, besides, I didn't want to re-litigate what occurred between us years before. I was aware, too, that a memory needs something like a nimbus to survive. To survive and to endure. That to end a memory, to render it a memory no longer by exposing it, risks making the old sequences progressively smaller. That, if we spoke of the quarrel, no longer would there be a quest for whatever beauty or totality or secret might be mined there. I was aware, too, that any discussion of what occurred so long ago between us might dispossess me of my own life. Still, I asked him anyway, knowing that the memory might be shattered by doing so.

—Do you remember, rabbi, we had a quarrel?

He shifted his weight. His eyes widened. And he stepped backwards.

—Been nice talking to you, he said, and he softly shook my hand, before turning to walk down the hallway and disappear though the air-conditioned shadows, as if the outside and the inside of time were converging, with each step his pedometer ticking.

Already as I steered the car onto the Loop and drove north, the discontinuities of the encounter fell away, floating in and out like vibrations of light, the sky fraying in the distance behind me toward Galveston Bay. Had I looked at my face in the rear view mirror, I might have thought, that's not me. Must be somebody else, shackled to some other existence—hollowed, furrowed, heart beating too fast, trouble with breathing. But also that face seemed to contain preparation for the future to come when time reels down, hovers and pirouettes, then twirls, and comes to rest, bristling with mystery—windblown, exuberant, abandoned, trembling, but tranquil.

Perhaps the potential for our lives is always rooted in the dark ground. It grows from twinkling points of particularity. We climb down to retrieve it or it rises to the surface like a bubbling of light, then brightens and becomes evanescent.

My future had become my past, like a small lamp burning continually.

It hurt to think of leaving home again. It was like being flayed and knowing that, at any moment, with the next flood and the last teardown, word will come that the place is gone. Surely we all expect to be remembered. Our memories need each other, even if I'm now relegated as the long forgotten past. We need to know we exist in the memory of someone else, just as they do in our own. I like to think a social DNA is in play. We did these things, on these streets, under these skies, all of us, and that exists always, even if unseen.

And yet with so many kaleidoscopic images knotted in my head over decades, it's impossible to know what's original anymore. So I must again invent the story of my life. As everyone does. To hear the whispered messages. To smell the wind, like a familiar stain. To see that I am a man who watches the clouds and longs for the skies. Not everything is possible again. But new possibilities are out there. I have an extreme desire to hold onto this feeling. *Texas* is my word for it.

Something happens to the mind when it comes to a

reckoning. It's like tasting your blood and perhaps, we think, it's the last time we'll have these thoughts. It's like you've been chasing victory, and the chase is always a delirium. It requires no amplification, nor forgery. If anything, the vision intensifies like a myth. I know that when we are separating from what we think we understand about life in order to explore what we don't understand, we experience a range of apprehensions, even it if means admitting the repudiated and accepting the tragic. That's the nature of the pursuit of home. Isn't it? To accept that even in the most familiar realms of one's existence, you are not a master of all its meanings.

Immediately, I felt new questions. Is it resolved? How can it be when the place so inhabits me?

I studied the ribboned clouds near the horizon so that all these feelings, like a soul, might depart my body, and I would not be distracted by the last look upon the land. All over the city the fading light was sheltering behind the houses, in the trim hedges, curling at the ends of long driveways, in the shadows of garages and parked cars. You could get lost in a sky like that, as if you were flying with your arms at your sides like a figure in Chagall above the rooftops and high rises and roadways. You could fade into the drifting clouds over the tree line and glass towers and radio spires, the antennae of so many cars and trucks picking up the pop songs and country western hits and radio preachers, with the traffic speeding and slowing and crossing, or inching forward under the overpasses, or curving at high speeds, the billboards illuminated.

I drove toward the territory plunging in the west. I knew nothing would survive of what I'd just desired. The horizon was an unfathomable intricacy, a stretch of clouds breaking loose, slipping into strands, flowing freely. The slender light falling, lost forever, under a loose and steady sky.

ABOUT THE AUTHOR

David Biespiel is a poet, memoirist, and literary critic. He is the author of eleven books, among them *Republic Café*, *The Education of a Young Poet*, *The Book of Men and Women*, *A Long High Whistle*, and *Every Writer Has a Thousand Faces*. A contributor to *The New Republic*, *The New Yorker*, and *Slate*, he has won a number of awards for his writing, including Lannan Foundation, National Endowment for the Arts, and Stegner fellowships, two Oregon Book Awards, the Pacific Northwest Booksellers Award, and he has been a finalist for the National Book Critics Circle Balakian Award. He has taught at Stanford University, University of Maryland, George Washington University, and Wake Forest University. He is the founder of the Attic Institute of Arts and Letters and Poet-in-Residence at Oregon State University.